ANTONY HOPKINS

Sounds of Music

A study of orchestral texture

J. M. Dent and Sons Ltd
London, Melbourne and Toronto

First published 1982
© Text, Antony Hopkins
© Line illustrations, Constance and Brian Dear

Printed in Great Britain by
Billing and Sons Ltd
Guildford, London, Oxford and Worcester

for J. M. Dent & Sons Ltd
Aldine House, 33 Welbeck Street, London W1M 8LX

This book is set in 10 on 12pt VIP Times
by D. P. Media Limited, Hitchin, Hertfordshire

Music examples prepared by Tabitha Collingbourne

British Library Cataloguing in Publication Data

Hopkins, Antony
  Sounds of music.
  1. Musical instruments
  2. Orchestra
  I. Title
  781.91   ML460

ISBN 0-460-04447-8

Contents

Acknowledgments

The author is grateful to the following publishers for permission to reproduce copyright material.

Boosey & Hawkes Ltd: Extracts from Britten's Four Sea Interludes, op. 33a, in chapter 13.

Ernst Eulenburg Ltd: Extracts from Brandenburg Concertos III and IV on pages 24 and 25.

Oxford University Press: Extract from Walton's Symphony No. 1 on page 78.

To Janet,
in gratitude for all her labours on my behalf

Prelude

I begin with a memory from boyhood days, clear as a photograph in my mind, yet one in which some of the faces seem to be looking away from the camera since the figures are mostly unidentifiable. We are in a group of four or five, all much of an age, by which I mean that period when one begins to take oneself and one's opinions seriously, without actually having much grounds for doing so. The scene is the forecourt of Berkhamsted Station; we are presumably waiting for someone to arrive rather than depart, or else we would be on the platform. If many of the visual details have the maddeningly elusive quality of a remembered dream, the content of the conversation remains amazingly fresh in my mind even after a gap of over forty years. For little better reason than to pass the time, a member of the group begins one of those verbal games which children still enjoy. 'What's your favourite instrument, then?' The question goes the rounds; not surprisingly I opt for the piano, while the son of the bandmaster (whose inherited aptitude is such that he can play a dozen instruments tolerably) speaks up eloquently for the clarinet, on which he has revealed a precocious mastery since the age of ten. Other replies, hesitant or non-committal, fail to contribute enough to sustain our flagging interest. Then from the one girl in the group comes the conversational bomb whose reverberations have echoed through my mind ever since. 'Well,' she said, with an air of firm authority that boded ill for any future husband, 'I don't care what you all say, my favourite instrument's the *orchestra* . . .' To a man we rejected this as a typically feminine evasion of the point; the orchestra was not an instrument; to regard it as one was clearly cheating. Heatedly she maintained that it was, that one man, the conductor, played upon it just as an organist played a great assembly of differently voiced pipes, that composers wrote for it not as a motley group of instrumentalists but as one immeasurably rich source of varying tone-colours. Naturally I did not allow myself to admit that her arguments in any way convinced me, but the mark was made. Ever since that brief and seemingly rather foolish discussion I have acknowledged the wisdom and perception of her view; the orchestra is indeed an instrument, one which composers have used over the centuries as a vehicle for the expression of every mood, from the most sublime to the most frivolous. How they have done so, how blended its

1

multifarious tones, how extended its capabilities I shall attempt to explain in this book.

Before beginning a detailed exploration of the orchestra, let us try to imagine what the art of composition involves. Although we may have no aptitude for painting, most of us can identify fairly easily with an artist at work. There he stands, a blank canvas in front of him, his subject (be it a landscape, a still-life or mayor with chain) nicely in view. With a few deft strokes a rough outline appears, often in a sequence that is surprising to the ignorant observer but which nevertheless soon becomes the recognizable skeleton of a painting. After that it is a matter of time and the application of skill and imagination; given the patience, we can watch the whole process and, even though we may sometimes feel the choice of colour surprising or perverse, we *understand*.

Our conception of the writer, whether novelist, poet or historian, is rather less clear. The historian or biographer, we feel, must have to do a great amount of research, something that cannot be all that different surely from mugging up a subject for an exam – just reading, taking lots of notes and then regurgitating on the day. Naturally we realize there's a bit more to it than that, but given the dedication and industry (and a reader's ticket to a good library) it's conceivable that one might knock off a tolerably convincing account of, say, naval warfare in the nineteenth century if one felt so inclined. Novelists and poets of course one regards as more 'creative', though even novelists say they are doing research when they want an excuse to go and have a nice holiday in Mexico. Has it not been said that everyone has one good novel inside him if only he could write it down? To this extent, then, we tend to feel that arts that we can *see* being accomplished (painting, sculpture, acting, dancing) are not totally unattainable. Given the chance when young, we say in our Walter Mitty-ish moments, we too could have done that. Even the writer's art is not beyond understanding; most of us wrote a poem or two at school – may even have had it published in the school magazine, or had it read out to the whole form, blushing the while. But when we come to composition we move into altogether more intangible realms.

In a sense the child humming to himself as he plays a solitary game is composing, but he does so formlessly and without the multi-layered dimension of harmony that true composition involves. Composers are born, not made, the first indication being what might colloquially be described as 'noises in the head'. I have sometimes defined composition as 'the identification of sounds half-heard', a definition which describes fairly accurately my own experience. It is a lonely business in which the ears have to develop the uncanny knack of listening inwards. Inside the brain, as though in some acoustic shell, sounds lurk; they must be tracked down, captured, brought out to be examined. Often they are then rejected; the painful dismissal of unwanted harmonies takes far longer than the gratified acceptance of the one sound that seems totally appropriate to one's need. For the modern composer the problems are enormously magnified by the sheer quantity of music already written. 'It's been done before' is the depressing motto that confronts him time after time as he searches for a thread to lead him out of the sonic labyrinth of the mind. Even so, material and tone-colour usually emerge as one; when Brahms chose to start his Piano Concerto No. 2 with a phrase for solo horn, I am positive that he never for a moment considered whether it might sound as well or better on a clarinet, a bassoon, a viola, a cello, the first violins or a cor anglais. Though each is a perfectly practical alternative, it is also an unacceptable alternative; the horn lends the phrase not only stature but the quintessentially romantic character epitomized by Byron's *Childe Harold*.

Now clearly this is not the case with every note in an orchestral score; themes *are* transferred from one instrument or group of instruments to another, although to do so invariably leads to a change of character. As for accompanying figures, the 'padding' as one might unkindly describe it, there are many alternative possibilities open to a composer; his ultimate choice will be dictated by considerations as varied as practicality (the size of the orchestra), emotional content (sombre or light-hearted), nationality (that concept of sound we call Germanic or Bohemian, etc.) or simply personal temperament. However, there are so many complexities in the average symphonic score that even to suggest that it can be reduced to themes and accompaniments is misleading. To a certain extent there is a parallel between that artist I spoke of and the composer; long after the observer is ready to congratulate the painter on what seems to him an adequately finished canvas, the artist will continue to touch in innumerable little dabs of extra colour, each of which will in due course be seen to be justified. Similarly the composer, whose first draft will normally be a somewhat illegible 'rough' score with many a cryptic sign that only he can decipher, will, on making the fair copy, add many a little touch, ranging from a substantial counter-melody on the woodwind to an isolated but effective note on the celesta.

To pursue the analogy further, instrumental sound is to the composer what his palette is to the artist; indeed there are words that are applied in common to both arts – do we not speak of tone-*colour* in a piece of music or of the *rhythm* in such-and-such a painting? Just as colours convey readily identifiable emotional characteristics, so does tonal colour (*timbre*) have what one might term a vocabulary of association. It is an almost unavoidable cliché that fanfares are best suited to brass instruments, that low soft drum-rolls give an air of menace, that rapid flute passages are mercurial, that wide-spaced quietly sustained string chords suggest peace and stillness. The mere existence of such well-established devices serves as a challenge to the composer to find new ways of achieving comparable effects: the greater the credit, then, to Beethoven for *avoiding* the use of timpani at the start of the storm in the 'Pastoral' Symphony, or to Michael Tippett for announcing the arrival of the Ancients in his opera *The Midsummer Marriage* with a fanfare not even on muted trumpets but on a celesta. (A magical sound for a magical race.)

Since some composers are gifted with far greater facility than others (not necessarily a virtue), it is dangerous to make too detailed an analysis of the processes of composition; all the same, if we discount the factor of time that distinguishes the composer who writes an opera in three months from the one who takes three years, certain generalities must be so common as to be virtually universal to them all. The starting-point must clearly be the decision as to the genre of the work – string quartet, piano sonata, oratorio, symphony, song-cycle or whatever it may be. Even so basic a decision as this will have its effect on the creative subconscious. As I have sometimes said, 'One sends an order down to the kitchen, and in due course something comes up through the hatch.' By some mysterious means, what comes up is usually germane to the order; in other words, if a string quartet is planned, the material that emerges, in however insubstantial a form, is unlikely to be pianistic or vocal in its idiomatic implications. These first intimations may be genuinely of use or they may be only pointers that in turn provoke other and more productive ideas. (Beethoven's sketch-books are the most eloquent demonstration of how dross may be turned to gold; most of his first drafts are so banal that any normal musician would have rejected them out of hand.) Fortunately ideas breed; once the first moves are made, the creative force tends to gather impetus. It is at this stage, though, as the vision of the whole movement begins to clarify, that what I describe as the 'identification of sounds half-heard' comes to the fore. Perhaps because deep in the subconscious there is a tumult of ideas waiting to escape to the surface, one can experience a sort of confusion, as though different sounds are demanding to be heard at once. One reason why a sonic structure is so useful – be it eighteenth-century fugue, nineteenth-century sonata form or twentieth-century serialism – is that it helps to provide a discipline in the organization of sound. (The exposition of a fugue almost writes itself once the knack has been acquired.) As the textures grow more complex, embracing many layers of sound simultaneously, so the composer must grow ever more competent in his technique, in his ability to imagine with precision what this silent clamour within will actually sound like when it is given instrumental life. Occasionally he may gamble or guess; usually he will know with some confidence that here the violas will need reinforcement from the clarinets or that there horns straining at the top of their compass will sound more exciting than trumpets having a relatively easy time. While some of this expertise may be ascribed to training, some to observation, experience, or learning by precept, in essence it should be intuitive and personal, the composer's signature in sound. It would be foolish to deny the importance of melodic shape and harmonic progression, whether the subtly exotic pattern of a Bartók theme or the sensuously evocative chords in Debussy. Of course these play an enormous part in giving a composition a clear identity; yet the fact remains that Brahms, Tchaikovsky and Dvořák can write symphonic movements for orchestras that are identical in personnel while still managing to conjure from them sounds that are unmistakably their own. Elusive phenomenon though it may be, I hope in these pages to cast some light on it. First we must discover something about the origins and emergence of the orchestra itself, an evolutionary process that took the better part of two centuries in what we now call Europe, infinitely longer if we cast our net back to the earlier civilizations of ancient times.

Part I

1

The False Dawn

It would be gratifyingly tidy if it were possible to trace a direct evolutionary path from those instruments familiar to us today back to their earliest ancestors, a sort of musical Darwinism whereby one could state with absolute conviction that the instrument so clearly depicted in relief on the walls of the tomb of Paatenemheb in Egypt, Eighteenth Dynasty, *c.* 1400 BC (see opposite), did ultimately evolve into the harp we see in the modern concert hall. Tempting though it may be to sustain such an argument, especially when presented with such persuasive visual evidence, there is no chain of continuity that we can adequately establish. The fact is that despite the huge variety of instruments that have been developed by man over a period extending back to the Ice Age, the actual means for creating sound are surprisingly limited. One can set a string in vibration by plucking it, striking it or rubbing it; one can set a column of air into motion by blowing down or across a tube; or one can strike an object of some kind, preferably either hollow or metallic, since if it is solid it will lack resonance. Man's desire to make music appears to be virtually as old as the human race, as small bone-flutes dating back to the Glacial period clearly show. Even the most primitive races have cultivated sophisticated ranges of pitched drums made from sections of hollowed-out trees, animal skins or gourds. It is not surprising, then, that every civilization has developed roughly comparable families of instruments, wind, strings and percussion, irrespective of the immense isolation created by distance or the gulf of time. How can the makers of the flutes, bells and drums that we know to have existed in China more than 3,000 years ago have realized that in distant India, in the same period, other men of a totally different race and culture were also making flutes, percussion instruments and even plucked string instruments and reeds as well? Some four hundred years later, in mighty Babylon, King Nebuchadnezzar might have been entertained by a court-band that boasted brass, wind, strings (in the form of lyres and harps) and certainly some percussion, though what type the Book of Daniel fails to specify. It seems unlikely that the musicians played other than by ear, nor would the compass of the instruments have been likely to extend much beyond an octave. What is perhaps more surprising is the early correlation of music and science. The

9

Harmonic Series (see page 42), which is still shown in every basic text-book on music to this day, was first discovered by the Chaldeans in the sixth century BC. According to legend it was in Chaldea that a young student named Pythagoras absorbed the theory and took it back to his native Athens, there to develop it into the basis of Greek musical philosophy.

In Ancient Greece, music sustained a division between the wind instrument (aulos) and the plucked string instrument or lyre (kithara). The more strident voice of the aulos was dedicated to Dionysus, while the dulcet tones of the kithara were deemed more apt for Apollo. Consequently that congregation of instruments which we think of as an 'orchestra' was not part of Grecian life. The Romans on the other hand, with their love of vulgar display, were much taken with large instrumental bands, the noisier the better, and even went so far as to devise an organ powered by water-pressure which would excite incredulity were it to appear in a Hollywood epic. (It should be remembered, though, that none of their brass instruments had valves and that therefore the sort of music supposedly played by cohorts of extras in cinematic reconstructions of Imperial Rome would have been completely impracticable. One presumes that during filming they trudge through the dust to records of Sousa marches, blowing manfully the while into their silent instruments.)

Apart from the timeless drum, the oldest instrument still in use today in its original form must be the Jewish *shofar*, the ram's horn used in solemn ritual; but there is also the *hazozra*, a short silver trumpet markedly similar to the famous trumpets found in the tomb of Tutenkhamun. It would have been on such an instrument that no fewer than 120 priests supposedly played at the dedication of Solomon's Temple, accompanied by lyres, harps, tambourines and cymbals. While the sound must have been impressive, the music itself can scarcely have consisted of more than an obsessional repetition of two or three notes. So far as is known, no system of musical notation had been devised at the time; however, ritual might be said to serve as a substitute for rehearsal and a degree of unanimity was probably achieved. At a guess I would imagine that a priest intoned a freely decorated improvised chant whose every phrase would be punctuated by the blare of instruments adding the equivalent to an Amen or Alleluia – literally a transcription of *halelû-yâh*, 'Praise to Jehovah'.

As the Roman Empire expanded to the point of dominating the known Western World, musical resources increased notably until a considerable range of instruments was available. There was a variety of trumpets and horns as well as wind instruments, some with a secondary pipe providing a drone bass, some without. Lutes, lyres and harps were in frequent use, as were a small assortment of percussion instruments. Even the *hydraulos* or water-organ proved to be capable of development. Here, then, was the basis upon which a rich instrumental heritage might well have been founded. Notation of sorts had been invented by both Greeks and Romans; quite an amount of knowledge concerning acoustic science had been acquired. Admittedly music remained monodic, single lines rather than a blend of harmonies. Yet, had progress continued on similar lines at a comparable rate, it seems likely that something closely resembling what we might call an orchestra could well have emerged by the fifth or sixth century AD. The knowledge, the materials, the craftsmanship, above all the essential delight in music that we might expect from a Latin people were all there; only a century or two more and how vastly different the history of music might have been.

It was not to be; the false dawn was followed by an era of darkness. With the collapse of the Roman Empire a few musicians doubtless made their way to northern parts, taking their instruments and their skills with them, there to become minstrels, valued only if they could play dance music to the peasantry. There was little cause for dancing. In the memorable words from Tippett's oratorio *A Child of our Time*, albeit with a less seasonal significance, 'The world turned on its dark side'. It would take several centuries for instrumental music to re-emerge in its own right. Longer still, some twelve hundred years, was the gap between the last death-throes of the Roman Empire and the birth of the orchestra in a form that we would acknowledge today.

2

From Darkness to Light

Man's innate desire to make music must have survived in some form even during the cultural twilight we speak of as the Dark Ages. While Christianity was certainly the saviour of Western civilization, its initial effect on instrumental music was extremely repressive. Austere times are reflected in an austere attitude to life; music continued to exist largely as a part of ecclesiastical ritual, either as unaccompanied singing or with such instruments as were available simply doubling the vocal line. When composers did begin once more to turn their skills to writing instrumental music they did so with a somewhat fatalistic approach, hardly ever specifying the instrumentation, but rather using some such phrase as 'fit for voices or instruments'. In other words the actual combination of instruments employed would depend entirely upon the availability of players. It is not within the scope of this book to dwell exhaustively on the subject of notation, the proper development of which was essential before any real progress could be made. What concerns us more is the gradual emergence of *families* of instruments, or 'consorts' as they were known. Thus a consort of recorders was designed to be a rough equivalent to soprano, alto, tenor and bass voices, as was a consort of viols of the various sizes (and therefore differing pitches) or of trombones, or sackbuts as they were more generally called. The earliest reed instruments, shawm, crumhorn and rackett, were somewhat raucous in tone and more suited to outdoor occasions. Much favoured was the 'cornett', in no way to be confused with the cornet of today since it was made of wood or ivory, having finger-holes much like those of a recorder and presumably boasting a comparable agility. (Monteverdi (1567–1643) complained bitterly that the cornett players in his opera orchestra were paid a higher stipend than he, so valued were their skills.)

With the emergence of 'consorts' of instruments one was able for the first time to have a tolerably well-blended sound from a group of players. If for practical or even for artistic reasons it was thought politic to mix strings and wind together, the resulting group would be called a 'broken consort'. During the fifteenth century such mixtures became increasingly exotic and might indeed be referred to as orchestras of a sort even though the art of orchestration, in the sense of the subtle blending of differing tone colours,

12

had not been thought of. Instruments either played antiphonally with one group answering another or, more commonly, together, moving in more or less parallel lines. Bagpipes of various kinds were played by the country-folk of many nations, percussion instruments also having an international standing. By 1547 instruments had become a rich man's status symbol, for in that year it was noted that King Henry VIII had amassed a collection of no less than 272 wind and 109 string instruments. A clear division had formed between religious and secular music even though instrumental resources were freely used within the church. However, there was still no real 'orchestral' music as such; for that we need, paradoxically enough, to go to the opera-house, for it was there that the development of a true orchestral sense began. This is hardly surprising since it was in the theatre that dramatic effects, such as storms or battles, were required.

Although much credit must be given to Giovanni Gabrieli (1557?–1612) for his adventurous excursions into purely instrumental music, the fact remains that his use of antiphonally contrasted groups of instruments has a haphazard look about it at times that suggests that circumstance rather than aural imagination was a decisive factor. For instance, in some of his *Sacrae Symphoniae*, we find distinctly weird grouping, as when one cornetto, one viola, one tenor trombone with tenor and bass singers exchange phrases with a section consisting of cornetto, viola, *three* trombones and alto voice. Gabrieli appears to have had no standard orchestra, his predilection being for brass (from two to six trombones), cornetti, violas (or viola d'amore) and an occasional bassoon. It is to Monteverdi that we must look if we are searching for the first significant orchestrator of music in the generally accepted meaning of the word. Although tragically a number of his later operas were lost or destroyed during the sack of Mantua in 1630, enough has remained to show his truly revolutionary feeling for sound as a composer's most imaginative resource. So far as we know, he wrote no purely instrumental pieces, but his operas and large-scale church compositions show him to have been a master of musical imagery. Unlike so many of his predecessors, he specified his instrumental requirements very precisely; on the second page of the contemporary score of *Orfeo* (1607) we find the detailed list of the composition of his orchestra shown on page 14.

Although this must undoubtedly be classified as an orchestra, it bears hardly any resemblance to even the Handelian orchestra of little more than a century later. Furthermore, Monteverdi seldom requires all his instruments to play together; indeed when he does so he goes back to the old pot-luck system of failing to specify who should play what. On the other hand he selects most carefully small groups to accompany the various arias or set-pieces so that, despite the relatively static harmonies and slow pace, the ear is constantly beguiled by changes of tone-colour. The voices are mostly accompanied by the keyboards, but the introductions to each scene and the ritornelli that punctuate the arias are scored with a precise ear for their

13

36 players in all, though it is quite probable that the trombones and trumpets were played by the same instrumentalists.

{

Two keyboard instruments of the harpsichord family, i.e. *not* organs.

Two double-basses.

Ten viols played-on-the-arm (*Viole de Brazzo* – which probably means both descant and tenor viols).

One double-strung harp.

Two treble violins.

Two arch-lutes (*Chitarroni* – a sort of bass guitar with a double set of strings).

Two organs with wood pipes.

Three bass viols.

Four trombones (sackbuts).

One regal (a portable reed organ).

Two cornetti.

One piccolo flute.

One normal trumpet.

Three muted trumpets.

effect. Thus we find such carefully constituted groups as 'Two violins with Bass viol and Chitarroni' or 'Viols, Bass-viols, Double-Bass and Organ'. For the scenes in the underworld he uses cornetti, trombones and the regal, saving their darker hues for a special effect, just as Mozart was to do with his trombones in *Don Giovanni* 180 years later.

If Monteverdi in Italy led the way, others were soon to follow; in France Lully (1632–87) and later Rameau (1683–1764) were to prove astonishingly inventive and daring in their operatic scoring, while in England Purcell (1659–95) became possibly the greatest theatrical composer of the seventeenth century.

The most significant step forward in the development of something like a standard orchestra came not with the *invention* of the violin (in about 1550), but with its increasing *availability*. Just as in the eighteenth century the harpsichord was gradually displaced by the piano (or fortepiano as it was initially called), so in the seventeenth century the viols were made obsolete by the violin, viola and violoncello. Several writers at first expressed their disapproval of the violin, complaining of its harsh shrill tone; but it soon proved its worth, both in the opera-house and the aristocratic households, where music was regarded as an essential perquisite to a civilized life-style. For a time viols and violins managed to co-exist; Dowland's *Lachrimae* (1604) are scored for 'viols or violins'; however, by the mid-seventeenth century a string orchestra of violins, violas, cellos and double-basses had become part of the establishment of every opera-house, with flutes, oboes, bassoons, trumpets, horns and drums being added as required or as finance dictated. For a time the more archaic instruments such as the lute and chitarrone lingered on, probably out of a sentimental reluctance to get rid of players who had given loyal service.

Of recent years musicologists have made valiant efforts to recapture the authentic sound of early instrumental groups, and there are many recordings in existence which do give us a tolerable approximation to the tone-colours available to the seventeenth-century composer. What no musicologist can do is to give today's audiences seventeenth-century ears. Accustomed as we are to the perfect intonation and flawless technique of the great modern symphony orchestras, it is quite impossible for us to capture the sheer thrill that the Venetian public must have experienced at the first hearing of an opera by Monteverdi or his pupil Cavalli. The young of today are fascinated by the rich new world of sound opened up by electronic synthesizers, yet the novelty of such sounds can be no greater in impact than was the novelty of Monteverdi's 'orchestra'. When Monteverdi asked his string-players to play chords pizzicato – plucking the strings – or tremolo – rapidly reiterating a single note – he was calling for effects that were literally unheard of; audiences and performers alike were startled by such demands, so much so that the composer had some difficulty in persuading the players that it actually could be done. (Here indeed is a scenario that has been acted out many times over the centuries with casts whose central protagonists have ranged from Beethoven to Berlioz, from Wagner to Stravinsky, from Bartók to Stockhausen.) All the same it should be realized that the basic standard of string-playing was to remain relatively unenterprising. Although the '*Vingt-quatre violons du Roy*'[1] were regarded as one of the glories of the French Court from about 1610 onward, it is extremely unlikely that the players ventured beyond the third position, nor would their techniques of bowing have shown much facility. Their greatest asset was continuity of tradition coupled, presumably, with adequate time for rehearsal of a somewhat limited repertoire of dance-suites – galliards, pavanes, sarabands and the like. It was the Italians Corelli (1653–1713) and Vivaldi (1675–1741) who were to develop a more virtuoso style of playing; without their extension of violin technique, whose repercussions quickly crossed the national borders of Europe, it is possible that such masterworks as the Brandenburg Concertos of J. S. Bach might never have been written. Vivaldi was a mere ten years older than Bach, but the younger man studied the Italian's violin compositions assiduously, as we know from a number of transcriptions he made. Curiously enough, Vivaldi gained most of his practical experience from working with children, Bach from working with amateurs. For thirty-six years Vivaldi was in charge of music at a girls' orphanage in Venice; if any child showed exceptional talent, the master would dash off a concerto or sonata as a reward or as an incentive. Since obedience would have been

---

[1] A resident string orchestra of the violin family, but not only violins.

unquestioning, Vivaldi could experiment with any combination of instruments that took his fancy. Here was a true nursery for string-playing.

For Bach the way was harder; in his maturity at Leipzig (1723 onwards) he could draw on a professional 'orchestra' of a mere seven players – two trumpeters, two oboists, one bassoonist (an apprentice at that) and two violinists. That the trumpeters could double on horn or trombone was small consolation since it was normal practice at the time. For the rest he had to rely on amateurs, townspeople, university students or even schoolboys. The situation must have seemed unbelievable to him coming as it did after his previous appointment at Cöthen. There his prime concern had been instrumental music, supervising the Prince's private orchestra of eighteen players, eked out on occasion by state trumpeters and drummers. It was there that he received the commission for the six Brandenburg concertos, works in which he demonstrated a true mastery of writing for a small but virtuoso chamber orchestra. Since they are a significant monument in orchestral development, let us pause awhile in this admittedly perfunctory survey and look at them in some detail.

3

A First Landmark
The Brandenburg Concertos

Although a perfect ensemble or blend of instruments may be the aim of every conductor, the fact is that egalitarianism and music do not go together. In any group of players it is inevitable that two or three will be endowed with abilities superior to those of their colleagues. It is hardly surprising, then, that one of the first substantial instrumental forms to appear was the Concerto Grosso, in which a small group of technically more adept performers was placed in opposition to their less-skilled brethren. The select few were known as the *concertino* in contrast to the main body, or *concerto grosso*. The composition of the concerto was dependent largely on a realistic assessment of who the quality players were at any given moment. With the ever-present keyboard (*continuo*) to supply a supporting background of harmony, the concertino might consist of three string players, two oboes and bassoon or even a mixture of wind and strings. Whether consciously or not, composers were thus continuing to exploit the earlier conception of a 'consort' or 'broken consort', using it to make a marked tonal contrast to the general group of strings. The form had emerged from Italy, credit for its invention normally being given to Alessandro Stradella (1644–82) whose *Sinfonie a più stromenti* (1680) are genuinely orchestral compositions in their own right, as opposed to the operatic preludes to acts or arias which, in previous years, had been the mainstay of instrumental writing. Needless to say, the form was quickly appropriated by Corelli, Vivaldi and other lesser-known contemporaries. Incidentally it is worth mentioning that the terms sinfonia, sonata and concerto were virtually interchangeable at this time, their common bond being the absence of voices. (An introduction to a chorus or aria might be called a Sinfonia or Sinfonie, but only so long as the voices were silent.)

While Handel as a young man would undoubtedly have heard many a concerto grosso during his lengthy stay in Italy, Bach was indirectly indebted to a German composer called Georg Muffat (1653–1704) who, having been overwhelmed by a concert given in Rome under Corelli's direction in 1682, rushed hotfoot back to Salzburg there to publish his *Armonico Tributo*, a volume whose preface expounded in no less than four languages the delights of this new musical form. By the time Bach had attained his first important

17

musical post, the concerto grosso would have been widely accepted as a standard mode of composition.

Despite his love of choral music, it seems probable that Bach's employment by Prince Leopold of Anhalt-Cöthen was artistically the most satisfying period of his life. Between 1717 and 1723 he was in charge of a small household orchestra such as the nobility were accustomed to sustain. The Prince himself played the violin, the viola da gamba and the harpsichord and it is evident that music played an important part in his life. It was only natural, therefore, that he should cultivate musical friends, one such being the Margrave (Markgraf) of Brandenburg whose own private band was of a particularly high standard. While some scholars maintain that Bach simply dedicated the set of six concertos to the Margrave, having first written them for his own patron and employer, others would have it that the works were tailor-made to specifications given him by the dedicatee. It is a viewpoint I prefer myself, since the outstanding difficulty of some of the solo parts suggests that Bach had the individual prowess of some players in mind; perhaps there may even be an element of challenge in the works as though he were saying in the subtlest possible way, 'You may think your band is better than ours, but can they play this?'

The first concerto of the set is in the key of F major and is interestingly scored for two horns, three oboes, bassoon and strings; there is an additional part for a *violino piccolo*, a small violin which we would nowadays call a three-quarter size. It was tuned a fourth higher than the normal instruments and would have provided an effective contrast to them. (Monteverdi's 'two treble violins' (see p. 14) were almost certainly of the same type.) A keyboard continuo part is indispensable, although, as was the custom, only the bass line is given, the performer being presumed competent to provide the harmonies himself according to a system of figuration.

The standard procedure in a concerto grosso was to begin with a tutti in which everybody played. The concertino group would then break free with music that was technically more brilliant; after some elaboration of this material, the main band would call things to order by a re-statement of the opening material, probably in the dominant, whereupon the concertino would again break away. The overall impression was thus one of alternating blocks of sound, not dissimilar to the contrasting of different manuals on an organ or harpsichord. Although Bach was thirty-six at the time, he had never before embarked on a work so clearly designed to exploit communal virtuosity among a group of players. Admittedly he had written plenty of instrumental music in his cantatas, but here was a very different proposition. It is interesting to see how varied were the solutions he adopted, each of the six concertos offering a quite individual approach to the problem of combining different instrumental strands.

Even the most casual glance at the instrumentation of the first concerto shows that he has three clearly defined tone-colours available: brass in the shape of two horns, reeds with the three oboes and bassoon, and strings – the harpsichord continuo acting as a sort of liaison between groups. The opening tutti might be described as something of a free-for-all, the horns declaiming one theme, the oboes another, both more agile and more complex than that of the horns, while the strings are given material that has something in common with both the other groups. The first significant breakaway occurs in bar 18, where the strings are given a phrase on their own; it is immediately matched by oboes and bassoon in bar 19 and then by horns and bassoon in bar 20. (Notice how Bach's ear tells him how much more appropriate a bass will be provided by a bassoon when the reeds or brass are prominent; similarly when the string concertino leads, cello and double bass play the bottom line.) By bar 27 a second general mêlée is joined, rather surprisingly in the relative minor instead of the dominant; furthermore, instead of being a re-statement of the opening themes it introduces new material, most noticeably in the horns. There is an air of general activity which reveals how essentially contrapuntal Bach's approach to composition was, much more so than is the case in his Italian predecessors. There is a distinct tendency for the score to be overloaded with notes, the oboes simply doubling up the violins in a way that Mozart or Haydn would have found distasteful in so complex a texture. Only twice in the first movement, and that briefly, does Bach begin to anticipate the art of orchestration as it was later to be understood. The moment is instantly recognizable; the violins and violas cease their bustling and provide a sustained central core of harmony; the semiquaver figuration in the bass at the *start* of each bar is matched by a corresponding figure in the horns at the *end* of the bar; the oboes build up harmonies in rising quavers during the first half of each bar, which in turn are balanced by descending quavers in the bass during the second half. Even though the bass line is overweighted by duplication of cello, double-bass, bassoon and continuo, the texture is momentarily clearer, the listener's task made easier by the simplification of outline.

Once we come to the slow movement we find music that is all the more effective for being so much more straightforward in its conception. Despite the rococo elaboration of the melodic line, the accompaniment remains discreet and subservient; even so, the tonal colour scheme is subject to ingenious change. Initially a solo oboe carries the melody, accompanied by gently throbbing chords from the strings, their harmonies subtly reinforced on the first beat of each bar by the two subsidiary oboes. At the fifth bar there is a change of sonority; the *violino piccolo* takes over the melodic line, the three oboes provide the pulsating harmonies, the remaining strings now add their support to the first beats. Next the melody is handed down to the cellos while violins and oboes alternate in a three-note phrase that is clearly meant to be a sigh. Not until the twelfth bar is there any interweaving of the melodic strands, the oboe initiating an extension of the original theme which is shadowed a beat later by the *violino piccolo*. With the added complexity that

19

this mingling of two decorative strands brings, Bach sensibly reduces the accompaniment to one chord to a bar, so placed as to give greater support to the weaker of the two solo instruments, the *violino*. The movement continues on these lines until, in its closing bars, it seems to disintegrate; the scoring here is particularly interesting, almost pointillistic in effect, each individual beat being allotted either to the harpsichord continuo, the three oboes or to the upper strings. These strangely isolated dabs of sound culminate in a chord on the dominant which all share equally. (Note that the horns are omitted from this tender and expressive Adagio.)

In the third movement we find similar techniques to those employed in the opening movement, the horns being especially athletic after their enforced rest. The mood is boisterous and vaguely bucolic, the horns lending an outdoor feeling to the scene. The ending is sufficiently rousing to make us feel that the concerto is complete. In fact there are two further movements, a Menuetto (with Trio suitably scored for two oboes and one bassoon), and a final Polacca for strings, which has in turn a second Trio scored most unusually for the two horns with all three oboes in unison providing a trumpet-like bass. It is in these final dances that Bach exploits the block contrasts between strings, wind and brass to the most positive advantage, denying his instinctive preference for either complex polyphony or an elaborately decorated solo line.

Looking back at the complete concerto, one could be forgiven for imagining it to provide a formula Bach might safely have used in the remaining five. Far from it. Although the Second Concerto is in the same key, F major, the lay-out is surprisingly different. As concertino Bach chose a strikingly diverse quartet – trumpet, flute, oboe and violin. Such a selection brings forcibly home to us his conception that even instruments so palpably different from each other could be regarded as interchangeable. This is an attitude no nineteenth-century composer could have accepted. Even in Purcell's day instruments were seen to have a clearly defined character, the 'tender, soothing flute' or the 'martial trumpet'. While Bach was certainly not indifferent to these characteristics, as his masterly choice of obbligato instruments in the Passions and cantatas shows, he seems to have felt that in a purely instrumental composition such as this it might be entertaining for each instrument to bring its individual timbre to the same theme in turn, rather than to devise music appropriate to its inborn characteristics. Once the opening tutti has given us a good taste of F major, the solo violin leads off with a cheerful theme accompanied only by the continuo. For two bars the combined forces reaffirm the tonality of F; it is then the oboe's turn to take over the violin's theme while the violin provides a nodding accompaniment. As though partaking in some formal dance in which the same steps are executed by constantly changing pairs of dancers, the flute now takes over the violinist's theme, accompanied by the oboe; as one might expect, the pattern comes to its logical conclusion when the trumpet has the theme, the flute now providing the accompaniment. The ingenuity with which Bach rings the changes on the various combinations available to him is remarkable, but it is composition for instruments rather than orchestration since the inherent natures of the four solo instruments are scarcely explored.

As in the First Concerto, the brass instrument is regarded as out of place in the slow movement; it is just as well, for the trumpet-player needs to conserve his strength for the daunting finale. This for once dispenses with the conventional opening tutti, beginning instead with a fugal theme for high trumpet that, along with many another passage in Bach, gives evidence of a skill that was to become strangely extinct within a matter of generations. It is one of the mysteries in music that the brilliant, florid style of trumpet-playing known as *clarino*, so wonderfully exploited by Purcell, Bach, Handel and their lesser contemporaries, should have vanished almost completely by the time of Mozart and Haydn. Even in Beethoven we cannot find a single trumpet part remotely comparable in difficulty to those written by Bach. It seems that during the late seventeenth and early eighteenth centuries a select group of players cultivated the special skills required to play with assurance and agility in the extreme upper register of the trumpet. Just as the medieval Guilds swore their members to secrecy about matters appertaining to their craft, so it appears did this embryonic musicians' union. Reluctant to pass on their secrets to a new generation, they preferred to let their expertise die with them, thus condemning brass players thereafter to virtually half a century of thoroughly boring parts.

At first glance the Third Brandenburg Concerto would seem to be the least interesting in orchestral colour since it is scored for a group of strings with no wind or brass to provide variety. A more careful look at the score shows us that Bach devised a completely original, possibly unique, disposition of his forces – three violin parts, three viola parts and three cello parts, with double bass and harpsichord giving the usual support to the bottom line. The three-note figure with which the movement begins proves to be astonishingly fruitful, its passage from one group to another being like a sonic game which Bach plays with the greatest dexterity. The first tutti, a mere eight bars long, ends with one of the rare unison passages, as though the players in the 'game' show that they are in agreement about the rules. The point made, they instantly split up and a rapid interchange begins between violins, violas and lower strings. Bach displays the ingenuity of a true master in keeping a fine balance between preserving the identity of the three groups while at the same time allowing subtle dialogues to take place. Every now and then he will thin out the texture so as to allow one solo instrument to predominate; for example in bars 47 to 50 the first violin has a tolerably athletic solo; in bars 51 to 53 the same figuration is taken over by the second violin while the other players sustain a discreet background that serves to remind us that these solo excursions are not irrelevant since they spring from the initial three-note pattern with which the movement began.

21

Although the bulk of the music is conceived as counterpoint in three tiers, there are enough instruments for Bach to produce richly sonorous harmony when he wishes, even though he may disguise a progression of chords by a rocking figure such as this:

The sound is magnificent, but one will not find anything like it in nineteenth-century music because later composers would certainly have felt the need to prolong the harmonic bone-structure with held chords in the woodwind, producing an effect somewhat comparable to that of the sustaining-pedal on the piano. As a foil to textures of this density we find other sections where the score consists almost entirely of three-note fragments scattered ingeniously between the violins and violas. The whole first movement is a masterly display of compositional technique, marvellously economical in material, marvellously expansive in the treatment of it.

The first movement is separated from the finale by two enigmatic chords which are certainly not meant to be played as written. This is no place for a hushed Amen. It was the custom of the time to encourage the art of improvisation, and the two chords may either be regarded as the framework for a cadenza from either the first violinist or the continuo player, or else as the conclusion (necessarily delayed) of a free improvisation from the keyboard which Bach would no doubt have supplied himself. As for the finale, it is a dance disguised as an exercise in counterpoint. A memorable moment occurs when the first viola is promoted to a position of eminence more usually occupied by the leader; finding itself in the topmost register it celebrates with the cheekiest of phrases while the violins, amazed at such presumption, remain rooted to a low C. The balance here is beautifully calculated; indeed the whole movement is a triumphant example of three-part counterpoint being given a new dimension by ingenious scoring.

Since it is hardly likely that Bach expected the Brandenburg Concertos to be played in continuity, too much importance need not be attached to the fact that Nos. 1 and 2 are in F major, Nos 3 and 4 in G major. Indeed Bach himself wrote an alternative version of No. 4 transposed down a tone into F major and substituting a keyboard for the solo violin. The essential point to make about the Fourth is its emphasis on lightness of texture. Here the concertino is a pair of recorders ('*Flutes à bec*', as he calls them) and a solo violin. In support we find the expected strings and continuo. But if we compare the opening of this concerto with its three predecessors, we will at once be struck by its transparency. The supporting strings often do little more than sketch in the fundamental harmonies, thus allowing the recorders every chance to be heard. The blend of recorders and solo violin would have been more satisfactory in Bach's time than in performances today, for the contemporary violin would have had gut strings and a flatter bridge; nor would the player have been likely to employ the forceful bowing technique that is now taken for granted. Nevertheless the solo violin part is formidable, as elaborate as a concerto in the more normally accepted sense. It is worth comparing a page of score from this work with one from the Third Concerto in order to see how different Bach's approach is when writing for an important solo part as opposed to a polyphonic web of equally matched sounds. (See pp. 24–5.)

Needless to say, the page is not always so sparse, but the whole first movement is exemplary in its care for balance. In this respect, the Fourth is the most expertly realized of the whole set, the concertino trio never being seriously threatened by the concerto grosso – or *ripieno*, as it is more commonly called. It is only in the finale that Bach creates a problem for himself since he chooses to write a robust fugue for which the gentle tones of the recorder are not too well suited. It is a theme to which oboes or trumpets would do better justice, and it is interesting to note that during the exposition of the fugue the solo violin plays in unison with his brethren, while the two recorders also give each other mutual support by playing together in their highest register. The most intriguing scoring comes immediately after the exposition when the three soloists are left on their own. Here Bach allows the two recorders to go their separate ways, giving the violin a note-spinning accompaniment that bears little resemblance to conventional fugal counterpoint. It is proper violin-writing, and in due course evolves into a display of some brilliant violinistic effects which none of the other performers attempts to emulate.

Most popular of the Brandenburgs is the Fifth, partly because of the sheer catchiness of its themes, partly because of the substantial keyboard part. Yet again Bach chooses a different combination of tonal colour for his concertino, the solo parts being allotted to flute, violin and harpsichord. It is worth mentioning that he specified a *flauto traverso* or transverse flute in this work. It is wrong to assume that the flute supplanted the recorder overnight; the two co-existed for some time, as did the harpsichord and fortepiano or the viola da gamba and the cello. As its name indicates, the transverse flute was held horizontally in the way familiar to us today, but its resemblance to the modern instrument was slight. Made of wood, most commonly box, but plum or cherry were also used, it was formed from four sections joined with rings of ivory. The equidistant finger-holes, similar to those on a recorder, were supplemented by a single key, giving the note D sharp. The instrument was set in the key of D, a decisive factor in Bach's choice of key for this work. It is believed that Bach actually saw a transverse flute for the first time in 1717 in Dresden, a mere four years or so before the composition of these concertos.

Brandenburg III

Brandenburg IV

The concerto opens with a joyous tune for the main body of strings; it has the habit of turning up a number of times, so it is properly called a *ritornello*, but surprisingly the three soloists show little interest, preferring to embark on more elaborate ventures of their own. Violin and flute tend to discuss shared ideas, the keyboard player being the most independent. This becomes most evident with the disproportionately long but irresistible cadenza given to the harpsichord towards the end of the first movement. It is a landmark in the early development of the keyboard concerto, being considerably more elaborate than anything in the solo keyboard concertos of Bach.

The slow movement is notable in that it is simply a trio sonata movement, the 'orchestra' remaining silent throughout. They are aroused from slumber by a 'hunting' fugue, bearing a remarkable but coincidental resemblance to 'A frog he would a-wooing go'. The exposition proceeds in the safe hands of the soloists for twenty-eight bars before the main body of strings joins in the hunt. Again one is made aware of Bach's keen ear for balance, the more florid passages on the harpsichord being accompanied by delicate chords well spaced from each other.

By contrast, the Sixth Concerto is a strange experiment in sonorities, being scored for lower strings only – two violas, two *viole de gamba*, cello, double bass and continuo. In fact even the word viola is misleading since Bach specifies *viole da braccio* – literally the arm-viol or tenor viol. Here, then, is absolute proof of the co-existence as separate entities of the members of the violin family used in the first five concertos and the viols employed in the Sixth. It seems unlikely that Bach regarded the final concerto of the set as a throwback, especially since his exploitation of wind instruments in the preceding works was so brilliant. In his eyes the concertos were indeed 'modern' music in its most adventurous sense. His decision to limit his tonal resources in this way might justly be compared to Stravinsky who, in the *Symphony of Psalms*, elected to omit violins and violas from his orchestra.

Of Bach's genius there can be no doubt, nor of the brilliance of this remarkable set of compositions; yet in the context of this book the question must still be asked: 'Was he a great orchestrator?' In terms of the Baroque era he certainly was, but that is begging the question somewhat. We have seen what a variety of tone colour he sought in his choice of solo instruments, but we have also seen that in making the thematic material completely interchangeable between those soloists he has to a certain extent annulled their individuality. It is interesting that this criticism applies least to the violin solo part in No. 4 and the keyboard part in No. 5; is it mere coincidence that Bach himself was most competent on both instruments and was therefore able to identify himself with them to a degree less possible with oboe, flute or trumpet? There are certainly times when he seems to have little consideration for his players, the wind especially. Oboes or flutes are often given no breathing space at all; admittedly in such cases they are usually doubling up a violin part and therefore may presumably leave out a note or two when asphyxia threatens. His trumpet parts are cruelly demanding even by the standards of the day. As to balance, his handling of the full orchestra in such works as the St Matthew Passion poses acute problems to the present-day conductor who tries in vain to blend oboes and violins or cellos and bassoons as they move relentlessly forward in sometimes imperfect unison. The moments of high drama, splendid though they may be, are not more ingenious in the use of orchestral sound than are those of Lully or Rameau in their operatic scores.

The Brandenburg Concertos may not be his greatest works – how could they challenge such supreme masterpieces as the B minor Mass or the St Matthew Passion? – but they can almost certainly be called his greatest 'orchestral' works. One surely does not have to seek far for a reason; whether they were written for his own patron's band or for that of the Margrave of Brandenburg, he was clearly writing for an outstanding group of virtuoso players. He could afford to experiment, to stretch resources, just as he did on a smaller scale in the works for solo violin or solo cello. Give a composer the means, and he will turn them to a worthwhile end. In that sentence we find perhaps the most fundamental truth concerning the relationship between composer and orchestra. For the art of orchestration to become something more than just allocating notes to different instruments, the orchestra itself had to come into being. The time was nearly ripe.

4

The Orchestra Emerges

Despite such examples as the accompanied melody in the slow movement of Brandenburg No. 1, the sum impression given by the set as a whole is of music in which counterpoint is the most natural medium for the composer's thought. This is rather less true of Bach's great contemporary, Handel, whose predilection for opera, with its consequent emphasis on a vocal line, led him to produce a less complex texture. That Handel was a master of counterpoint is not in doubt, but his youthful Italian sojourn left a lasting effect so that his music lacks the Germanic gravity so evident in Bach. (The *Daily Post* of 27 January 1729 refers to 'Mr. Handell, the famous composer of Italian music'.) Both composers in their rather different ways represent the summit of polyphonic choral and orchestral writing, yet during the latter part of their lives they were already becoming old-fashioned in their attitude to the orchestra. It is ironic that when we look for the most significant figures in the evolutionary period of the eighteenth-century orchestra they are mostly composers of minor importance, 'poor Yoricks' of whom we know far more through what has been written about them than through what they themselves wrote. Such names as Keiser, the brothers Graun, Wagenseil, Graupner, Pisendal, and Stölzel do not stand out in the average music-lover's mind as memorable figures; we may have seen them mentioned in a learned sleeve-note on a record of obscure orchestral music of the pre-Haydn era; here, though, were some of the leaders of a fundamental change in musical attitude. Aware, perhaps, that they could not outdo such great masters of polyphony as Bach or Handel, they groped their way towards a simpler style. Instead of the continuous interweaving of strands of music which we find in such works as the Brandenburg Concertos, they aimed for a texture in which one set of instruments would support the other. Thus if the melodic interest was in the woodwind, strings would provide an accompaniment which could be described as 'harmony in motion'. Meanwhile instruments such as horns and bassoons would supply a sustained core to the harmonies. Instead of the essentially linear approach inherent in counterpoint, there grew up a desire to blend sound, much as an artist blends two primary colours to produce another. Over a period of some fifty years the ubiquitous keyboard was banished from the orchestra, for its function of filling-in missing harmonies and acting as a liaison between different instrumental groups was no longer necessary. (Even so, Haydn directed the orchestra from the keyboard in the first performance of the 'London' symphonies in the 1790s.)

As has already been indicated, the opera houses gave orchestras the first semblance of a permanent home, but aristocratic patronage played an important part. Orchestral concerts on the public scale known to us today did not exist in the first half of the eighteenth century. Such orchestras of permanence as there were were attached to the innumerable royal or aristocratic households; their concerts were given in halls that might seat a hundred people at the most, of whom a few would be privileged outsiders, there by invitation rather than sufferance. Music-lovers of the middle-class formed societies such as the Collegium Musicum in Leipzig, whose concerts, with paid admission, were given at the Three Swans Inn.

It was in Mannheim that the most outstanding orchestra of the period was formed. Its director was Johann Stamitz (1717–57), a Bohemian composer whom the Elector Palatine engaged in 1742 to form an orchestra that was to become the musical wonder of Europe, surpassing even that of King Frederick the Great. (Some thirty-five years later Mozart was to hear the Mannheim orchestra; it made a profound impression on him and considerably influenced his orchestration in his final symphonies.) Stamitz and his successor Cannabich set great store on orchestral precision of a quality unusual at the time; he cultivated a wide range of tone including not only a genuine *pianissimo* but the new effects of *crescendo* and *diminuendo* that had scarcely been explored in concerted music. (In all fairness, credit should be given to the English composer Matthew Locke (1622–77) who, in his incidental music for Shadwell's *Tempest*, produced in 1672, indicated such dynamic contrasts as 'soft', 'louder by degrees', 'violent' and 'soft and slow by degrees'. As for the oft-repeated assertion that Rossini invented the crescendo, it is palpable nonsense; he simply exploited it to a degree hitherto unknown.)

It is impossible to give a precise date to the birth of the eighteenth-century orchestra which ultimately, in the hands of Haydn and Mozart, was to become an instrument of such pure delight. As early as 1722 the full score of an opera by Bononcini (1670–1755) was printed in London, where the Italian had established himself as Handel's great rival. As John Byrom (1692–1763) wrote:

> Some say, compar'd to Bononcini
> That Mynheer Handel's but a ninny;
> Others aver that he to Handel
> Is scarcely fit to hold a candle.
> Strange, all this difference should be
> 'Twixt Tweedledum and Tweedledee.

29

Bononcini's *Griselda* required the essential complement of strings which was the foundation of every orchestra together with pairs of flutes, oboes, bassoons, horns, trumpets and timpani (one player). It sounds an impressive enough combination and on paper is almost identical to the standard orchestra Mozart and Haydn used. (Clarinets, as we shall find, were not to arrive in the orchestra until the latter part of the century.) However, when we look at Bononcini's way of handling his resources it becomes apparent that he missed most of its potential. First and second violins are often in unison, possibly a reflection on their lack of numbers, and the viola parts are almost totally lacking in musical interest. It seems to have been a sad fact of orchestral life that viola players were universally regarded as third-class citizens; those who could not make the grade as violinists were happily relegated to the viola section and there was even an ancient orchestral players' joke that the viola desks were the last resting-place of horn-players who had lost their teeth. Composers were pragmatic enough to realize that poor players could be entrusted only with poor parts; it was many years before viola parts were to contain anything of much musical consequence, except in unison passages where their deficiencies could be submerged in the general welter of sound. As for the oboes and bassoons, Bononcini mostly used them as a reinforcement to the violin or cello parts. Flutes doubled the violins at the octave or again simply played in unison. Trumpets and horns added a martial bray when required, almost invariably accompanied in identical rhythm by the drums. In such orchestras a genuine tutti was rare since the oboes were often played by the flautists, the horns by the trumpeters; composers could choose one or the other but to be able to use all was a luxury.

In 1725 an organization known as *Le Concert Spirituel* was founded in Paris by Anne Philidor, primarily for the performance of sacred choral music with orchestral accompaniment. In due course it branched out to include symphonies and concertos, thus meeting a growing public demand for the new musical experience of hearing concerted music on a grand scale without the distractions of the operatic stage. By 1773, half a century after its foundation, this notable French orchestra had attained a strength of two flutes, three oboes, two clarinets, four bassoons, two horns, two trumpets, timpani, thirteen first violins, eleven seconds, four violas, ten cellos and four double basses. Even Mannheim could not compare with this; by the standards of the day it was a true symphony orchestra, considerably larger than the one Salomon was able to offer Haydn during his visits to London. Such a favourable balance was by no means universal and at almost exactly the same date (1771) the English historian Dr Burney reports that the orchestra in the splendid opera house at Naples had a string section of thirty-six violins (equally divided), two cellos and five double-basses, truly something of a bottomless pit! He fails to mention any woodwind but the general tendency in the latter part of the century was for orchestras to include a greater number of wind players than we would nowadays think desirable. Anything from three to six oboes and bassoons, three or four flutes and four horns was not regarded as excessive against a string strength of less than thirty players. Proportions were to change, and by the end of the eighteenth century a more or less standard format had emerged based on a Noah's Ark formula of pairs of woodwind and brass throughout, only the strings being allowed to multiply. Percussion other than timpani was a rarity used only for special effects, such as the depiction of war or distant and exotic lands. Triangle, cymbals, bass drum and bells were categorized as 'Turkish' music, a term that carried suggestions of the outlandish or even barbarous.

Before we leave the composition of the orchestra, the clarinets deserve a word to themselves. It is one thing to invent an instrument, another to make it generally available. J. C. Denner (1655–1707) made the first clarinet, probably as an improved version of a limited compass seven-holed pipe called the *chalumeau*, a term which is applied to the lowest register of the clarinet to this day. A glance at Denner's dates shows that he certainly did not live long enough to see his brain-child adopted extensively. Others (among them a J. Denner presumed to be a son) were to see its potential and during the course of the ensuing fifty years sundry improvements were made. The original instrument had but a single key; in time others were added, increasing the instrument's range and flexibility. In 1789 the brothers Stadler added a sixth key; both were fine clarinettists and it seems likely that Anton Stadler (1753–1812), a notable virtuoso, was the first to reveal the full possibilities of the clarinet to Mozart. His reward was a series of exquisite works, the Quintet K.581, the Concerto K.622 and the Trio for Clarinet, Viola and Piano K.498.

Of all orchestral instruments the clarinet's subtlety of nuance and smoothness of tone give it the closest resemblance to the human voice; Mozart seems to have felt this especially, and listening to his clarinet writing one often senses the sound of an imagined soprano in his mind. Incidentally, an interesting if not definitive confirmation of the superiority of opera-house orchestras comes with the realization that Mozart uses clarinets in most of his opera scores from *Idomeneo* (1781) onwards, but only in his last five symphonies (1782–8). Haydn, working with the limited resources available at the Esterhazy court, did not use clarinets in a symphony until No. 99 (1973), written for Salomon's orchestra in London. Both composers would have used a five-keyed instrument very different from the one we see on the concert-platforms of today, for Stadler's improved version was not generally available.

It may have seemed something of a laborious journey, but our basic cast is now assembled; it is perhaps a suitable moment to make a more detailed acquaintance.

5

Full Score

The sheer labour of writing music down is something of which the average listener remains happily unaware; in the days of quill pens, of parchment, of sand for blotting paper and illumined only by candlelight it must have been an appalling drain of energy. Some composers, the exceptional few, have the facility to work directly onto the full score, writing in all the instrumental parts as they occur. More often preliminary sketches and a rough score precede the copying out of a complete score, from which a set of orchestral parts must then be made, by either a professional copyist or a devoted student. In some cases poverty-stricken composers have even taken this exhausting task upon themselves when they have not been able to afford to have it done. One wonders sometimes how many extra creative years might have been afforded to the likes of Bach, Mozart or Schubert had the photocopying machine been invented in 1700.

Nowadays, with the exception of some modern experimental scores, a standard layout has been agreed, but it was not always so. For instance, even scores as late as Verdi's have violins and flutes at the top of the page, cellos and bassoons at the bottom – a not illogical arrangement from the point of view of pitch, but confusing when it comes to the identification of the four musical families of wind, brass, percussion and strings. Since in the art of orchestration the blending of sounds within these family groups became a prime concern, it was understandable that most composers should be drawn to a scheme that made such grouping easy to visualize. It became the general practice to place the woodwind at the top of the page, the brass below them, then the percussion plus any extras, such as the solo instrument in a concerto, a vocal part or the music for choir, with the strings showing themselves to be the foundation of the orchestra by their position at the bottom of the page. Here, then, is the basic layout observed by Mozart and Haydn in their later works. Let us work our way down the page, forgetting for the moment the minor differences of compass between the instruments of the early orchestras and the more familiar ones of today.

The Woodwind

The **Flute**. The sound is produced by blowing across a small hole near the stopped end of what is in effect a (metal) pipe some two feet in length; shallow saucer-shaped keys designed to fit the finger-tips enable the player to change the pitch. The instrument is assembled from three pieces or 'joints', the working compass being three octaves.

(Some modern flutes have one extra semitone lower, going down to B natural, while skilled players can find an extra two semitones at the extreme upper end.) The upper register is shrill and penetrating, the lower somewhat breathy. No more beautiful demonstration of the flute's most seductive qualities can be found than the opening passage of Debussy's *Prélude à l'Après-midi d'un faune*. Its other great asset is agility, coupled with brilliant articulation.

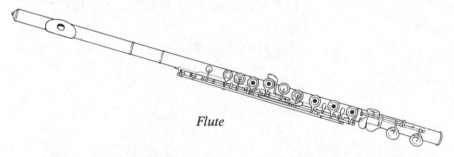

Flute

There are several other members of the flute family, most notably the **Piccolo**; as its name implies, it is simply a small flute designed to play an octave higher than the normal flute. In spite of its diminutive size its tones are piercing enough to be heard above the full orchestra, as Beethoven vividly demonstrated in the Storm movement of the 'Pastoral' Symphony. The piccolo is normally played by the *second* flautist; the notes being written an octave lower than the actual sound to save a perpetual clutter of *leger* lines. Its working compass is

but the extreme top notes are hard to produce.

Piccolo

A good deal rarer is the **Alto Flute** (also known as the Bass Flute or the G Flute). It is what is known as a transposing instrument; in other words, the written note middle C,

which the player reads and fingers exactly as a normal flautist would, actually produces the *sound* of a G a fourth below. Any flute-player can play an alto-flute at first acquaintance since both fingering and written compass are identical; he must simply learn not to be confused by the unexpectedly low tones he is producing. The tone is ravishing, especially in the lower register, and was used to memorable effect in the lullaby at the beginning of Act II of Benjamin Britten's opera *The Rape of Lucretia*.

The **Oboe** (Earlier: Hautboy or Hautbois). The tone of the oboe is produced by blowing air through the narrow aperture between two cane 'reeds'. Made of ebonite or rosewood, it is conical in bore with a widened 'bell' at the bottom end. At the top is a short piece of metal tube called the staple into which the reeds, bound together with waxed thread, are inserted. As with all the modern wind instruments there is a complex arrangement of keys and rods to enable the player to produce the wide range of notes of which the instrument is capable without changing the basic position of his hands – playing by remote control it might be called. The compass is less than the flute's, the top notes being rather thin and precarious to all but the most expert player.

There are innumerable examples of expressive oboe solos, but none better than the opening of the slow movement of the Brahms Violin Concerto.

Oboe

Like the flute, the oboe has some relatives of which the best known is the **Cor Anglais**, in effect an alto oboe. It has been suggested that 'anglais' is a misnomer for 'anglé' or angled, since the most obvious difference between

35

the two instruments is the pronounced crook in the upper portion and the more protuberant pear-shaped bell. Like the alto flute, it is a transposing instrument, the part being written a fifth higher than the actual sound. If the player uses the oboist's fingering for middle C, the sound produced will be the F below. The compass is over two octaves,

but as in the case of most of the orchestral 'lower brethren', the upper notes are seldom used since they can be more effectively played by the oboe. Notable solos include the main theme from the slow movement of Dvořák's Symphony 'From the New World' and *The Swan of Tuonela* by Sibelius. The instrument is sometimes 'doubled' by the second oboist, but more properly an extra player is employed.

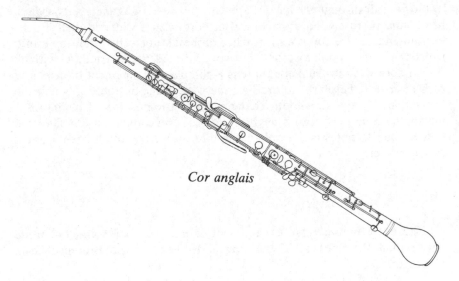

Cor anglais

Other variants of the oboe favoured by composers of J. S. Bach's era were the *oboe d'amore* and the *oboe da caccia*, although whether either one was especially potent as an instrument of love or of the chase is open to speculation. They have now fallen into disuse except in performances where historical authenticity is valued.

The **Clarinet** is an instrument whose origins we have already explored (see page 31). Unlike the oboe it has a single cane 'reed', the mouthpiece being somewhat like a beak, part of which is flattened to form a support for the reed, which is bound into place by a metal ligature. The reed rests against the lower lip of the player, but sufficient freedom of movement must be allowed for it to vibrate and set the air column in motion. Like so many of the orchestral family, the clarinet is a transposing instrument, although clarinets 'in C' – i.e. non-transposing – were tried in the first half of the eighteenth century. What is unusual is that it continues to exist in two separate forms, the clarinet in B flat and the clarinet in A. This is a practical way of ensuring that the clarinettist does not have to play in tonalities with an excess of sharps or flats. The B flat instrument transposes down a tone (written C sounding B flat) while the A clarinet transposes down a minor third (written C sounds A). Since passages with a superfluity of sharps or flats are awkward to finger, the player can, by changing from one instrument to another, simplify some of the technical problems involved. For example, suppose the orchestra is playing a symphony in E major; to use a B flat clarinet would mean writing the part a tone higher, in F sharp (or enharmonically G flat) major, whereas transference to an A clarinet would put the written part into the much more straightforward key of G. Similarly a composition in A flat major would be simple on the B flat clarinet (written part in B flat – key signature, two flats) and downright awkward on the A clarinet (written part in B major – key signature, five sharps). Needless to say, in music lacking any consistent tonality the choice is immaterial, the general preference being for the B flat instrument. The compass of the two instruments varies inevitably, although it is similar to the eye. Written thus:

it will sound a tone lower, D—B flat on the B flat instrument, a minor third lower, C sharp—A, on the A.

Although the clarinet is capable of the most agile passages, especially in delightfully fluid-sounding arpeggios, it has an awkward area known as the 'break' from

Not only does it present problems of fingering, but there is a distinct loss of tone quality, which causes the prudent composer to avoid writing solos in this part of the instrument. There are many brilliant solo clarinet parts in the orchestral repertoire – the *Dances of Galanta* by Kodály, the *Capriccio Espagnole* of Rimsky-Korsakov, or, in more romantic mood, the long clarinet solo in the slow movement of Rakhmaninov's Second Symphony.

Just as the flute has a shriller-voiced relative, the piccolo, so has the clarinet. A smaller instrument of higher pitch, the E flat clarinet (written C sounding the E flat a minor third above) is much used in military bands as a substitute for violins. It appears less frequently in symphonic music although

Berlioz makes effective use of it in the Finale of the *Symphonie Fantastique*, while its appearance in Strauss's *Till Eulenspiegel* is unforgettable in its cheekiness.

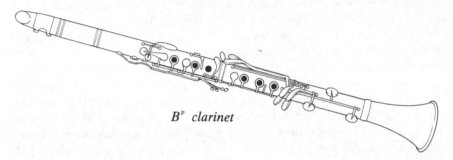

B♭ clarinet

A more regular member of the modern symphony orchestra is the **Bass Clarinet**, a large instrument with an unmistakably rich and mellow tone. Pitched an octave lower than the normal clarinet, it has a curved tube near the mouthpiece and an upturned bell at the lower end to accommodate its substantially greater length. The part is written a ninth higher than it sounds, giving a compass of

written, somewhat illogically:

Occasionally the parts are written in the bass clef nearer to the actual sound, but the more eccentric method shown above has its advantages in producing identical fingerings for the normal B flat clarinet and its bass partner. As with the cor anglais, the part is played by either the second clarinettist or, if the part justifies it, an extra player. Bass clarinet solos are not conspicuously frequent, although its tones are amongst the most tellingly effective in the orchestra. Most famous are the brief descending interpolations Tchaikovsky introduces in the 'Dance of the Sugar-Plum Fairy' from the *Casse Noisette* Suite.

While the Bass Clarinet was unknown in Mozart's time, there was an instrument with a somewhat comparable function, the **Basset Horn**. The name 'horn' is as misleading in this case as it is in cor anglais since neither instrument can conceivably be regarded as a member of the horn family. In fact it was the maker of the instrument who was named Horn (according to Forsyth; others attribute it to Mayrhofer of Passau); when he invented a Basset (or 'little bass') clarinet in 1770, he proudly attached his own name to

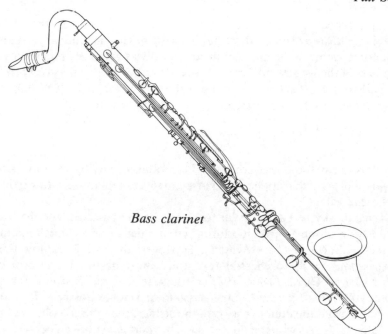

Bass clarinet

it, not anticipating the confusion that would then arise when the Italians translated the name into *corno di bassetto*. It might accurately be described as a tenor clarinet, and it has been argued convincingly enough that the Mozart clarinet concerto was originally composed for it. Its transposition is the only horn-like thing about it since, like the French horn in F, its part is written a fifth higher than it sounds. Its rather dark and serious timbre had a special appeal for Mozart, and he uses it in a number of works. Virtually obsolete in the orchestra of today, it has a useful compass:

Its nearest contemporary equivalent (also rare) is the Alto Clarinet.

The bass of the woodwind family is provided by the **Bassoon**, more usually referred to in scores by its Italian name, *fagotto*, to distinguish it (in abbreviation) from bass – for Double Bass. Like the oboe, the bassoon has a double-reed: owing to its considerable length (eight and a half feet) it has to be made with a U-turn, giving it the appearance which gained it its Italian name, *fagotto*, or 'a bundle of sticks'. The instrument is divided into five pieces in all; as can be imagined, the problems involved in designing the necessary keys and rods to enable the player's fingers to produce notes over a chromatic range of more than three octaves were considerable, and the modern bassoon has a lengthy evolutionary history behind it. During this

39

century, especially since the astounding bassoon solo at the start of Stravinsky's *Rite of Spring*, there has been an increasing tendency to explore its tenor register. In the nineteenth century it was generally regarded as the true bass of the woodwind family. It blends well with clarinets or horns and has perhaps too often been regarded as the orchestral jester. The compass is an extremely useful one, extending over a wide range:

Needless to say the upper notes can be produced only by the most skilled players, a proviso that applies to all instruments except those with keyboards or the equivalent.

Tchaikovsky had a particular fondness for the bassoon, whether in the serious vein of the Fourth and Fifth Symphonies or as a comic bass to the 'Chinese Dance' in *Casse Noisette*. However, the classic exploitation of the bassoons in the orchestral repertoire must occur in *The Sorcerer's Apprentice* by Dukas (1865–1935). It is here that the bassoons are most memorably joined by the **Contra-Bassoon** or **Double Bassoon**. It is to the woodwind what the double bass is to the strings, though it is neither as agile nor as versatile. As with the double bass, the part is written an octave higher than it sounds. Seldom entrusted with a solo, except for grotesque effects, it is capable of adding great richness to brass or wind chords in passages of a solemn nature. Brahms was a master of its use although one is sometimes unaware of its presence, so well does it blend with a nicely calculated mixture of trombones, tuba, bassoons and horns. It is the deepest voice in the orchestra, since not all double basses can descend to the low C.

sounding an octave lower.

Apart from a few exotic oddities such as the **Heckelphone** (a bass oboe), we have now completed our survey of the woodwind family. Saxophones would require a chapter to themselves, but they are still rarities in the symphony orchestra. Before moving on to the brass it is worth stressing that not all of the instruments mentioned were available to composers of the Mozart/Haydn era; even those that were were of a relatively simple design; all suffered from problems of intonation, as the great musical historian Dr Burney frequently recounts in descriptions of the many orchestras he heard during his musical travels. Substantial improvements had to be made, and the man primarily responsible for bringing them about was the great instrument-maker Theobald Boehm (1794–1881). Himself a flautist attached to the court orchestra at Munich, he was also a practical inventor of considerable skill. He needed not only the ability to work with the most precise accuracy in wood and metal, but also a practical knowledge of acoustic science. Beginning with the flute, which he virtually redesigned, he then turned his attention to the piano, producing an 'overstrung' instrument that was a notable impovement on its predecessors. His fame as an instrument-maker grew, and others turned to him for advice, Klosé and Buffet for the clarinet, Triébert for the bassoon; his principles were also applied to the oboe by Buffet, though with less success. Such was Boehm's reputation that even instruments with whose design he had little to do were named after him. Deservedly he was given pride of place, but it should not be forgotten that during the nineteenth century there was a continual demand for technical improvement in all instruments; even the string family was far from sacrosanct, the classically beautiful violins of Stradivari, Amati and their contemporaries being given longer finger-boards and higher bridges.

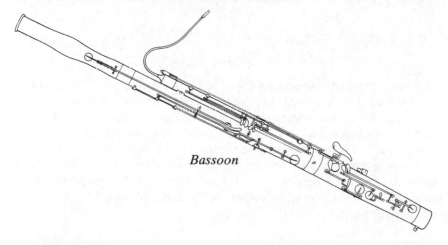

Bassoon

Such alterations were necessary to meet the ever more challenging demands of composers; nowhere could they have been more welcome than in the brass family, as we shall soon discover.

The Brass

Before we examine the instruments themselves, we need to understand the fundamentally different way in which brass instruments produce their sound. All woodwind instruments are basically pipes down which the player blows a column of air that vibrates within the tube, whether it be conical or cylindrical. The material from which the pipe is made – wood, silver, ivory, ebonite, etc. – is primarily responsible for the timbre or tone-colour of the instrument; but the change of *pitch* is accomplished by changing the hypothetical length of the pipe according to the elementary principles that 'short' equals 'high', 'long' equals 'low'. Compare the lengths of a piccolo and a bassoon and the point is made. The use of holes bored in the pipe enables the player to divert the air-column, thus changing its length and thereby the pitch. Other techniques such as 'overblowing' also come into it but need not concern us here.

With brass instruments the entire technique of sound production is based on different principles. As a boy I remember being amazed when the star bugler of the school band was able to play bugle-calls on a piece of gas-piping. Without a proper mouthpiece it would have been a painful exercise, but it revealed the acoustic truth that a hollow metal tube of adequate length has a sequence of notes built into it; this sequence is called the harmonic series and might be likened to the colour-spectrum in that it permeates all musical sound, individual tonal qualities being decided by the 'proportional representation' of harmonics within a given tone. The theoretical content of the harmonic series consists of a sequence of ever-diminishing intervals:

The notes marked with a cross (Nos. 7, 11, 13, 14), if audible, would not seem in tune with the tempered scale to which we have become accustomed.

These tonal components that go to make up the 'fundamental' as it is called – in this case the low C marked 1 – are known as 'overtones' or 'upper partials' and it is their strength or weakness that dictates the timbre of an instrument just as much as the material of which it is made. For example the clarinet emphasizes only the alternate overtones (3, 5, 7 etc) while the G string of the violin is mostly enriched by the 2nd, 3rd, 4th, 5th, 6th, 8th and 17th upper partials.

The **Horn**. Let us suppose now that instead of a length of gas-piping we equip our player with a brass tube long enough for him to be able to extract the low C indicated. (In fact it would have to be sixteen feet four and a quarter inches long, so it will be practical to coil it up into the familiar horn shape.) Having no reed to stimulate the vibration of air through the tube, he uses his lips, rather as a small boy does when imitating the sound of an aeroplane or car. In theory, and providing he has sufficient practice, he will be able to play all the notes of the harmonic series, although those in the upper register are extremely taxing. Note that every change of pitch is made by the player increasing or slackening the tension of the lips; the sound must be 'thought' in advance, the lip-tension or 'embouchure' precisely calculated. Since more notes of the scale are available in the upper range, early horn parts (before the invention of valves) tended to lie high. Theoretically it would be impossible to play any notes outside the harmonic series, although skilful players did devise a method of doing so by inserting a hand further into the bell of the instrument, thus shortening the overall length of the tube.

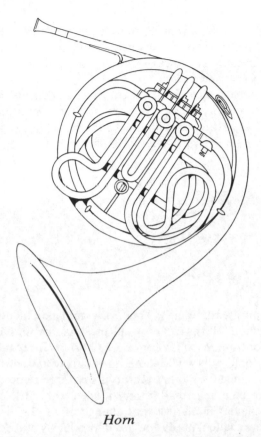

Horn

If, therefore, the composer required a different set of notes from those shown above, the only solution was to use a horn of a different length; since it was clearly impractical for a player to come to a concert armed with four or five rather cumbersome instruments, an ingenious alternative was devised in the shape of 'crooks', auxiliary lengths of tube which could be plugged in in such a way as to make a different harmonic series accessible. While this was clearly an improvement on the original 'natural' horn, it still denied the player anything like a full chromatic compass; it was the invention of the valved horn in the early nineteenth century which was to revolutionize horn-playing; one of the most intriguing indications of this occurs in the slow movement of Beethoven's Ninth Symphony, in one of whose variations the Fourth Horn is suddenly given a part that his colleagues were quite incapable of playing. It appears that the player was the proud possessor of one of the earliest two-valve horns; Beethoven, having seen it, obligingly gave him an opportunity to show what it was capable of!

Without going into too much mechanical detail, valves were simply a way of dispensing with crooks, diverting the air-column through different routes so that the player could at last play all the notes of the chromatic scale on the same instrument. If, for instance, the player needed the F sharp between harmonics 5 and 6 of the series shown, he could, by using valves, select either the 5th harmonic of a 'D' series or the 6th harmonic of a 'B' series; the end result would be the same.

Since it was the choice of instrument that decided which notes would be available to the player, horn-parts were habitually written as though in C major, regardless of the sound intended. If a symphony was in E flat major, the composer would simply specify 'Horns in E flat'; he might want the *sound*:

but he would write it down as:

The same phrase sounding in D major would look identical on the page, but the instruction 'Horns in D' would produce the required alteration in pitch. It was for this reason that once four horns were regularly included in the orchestra, composers would sometimes elect to have one pair in the main key of the movement, the other pair in a key more remote. In this way an episode in a foreign key could be introduced without losing the horns or involving the players in an awkward change of crooks.

Owing to the challenging difficulties of producing notes at either extremity of the instrument, players tended to specialize, first horn-players being adept at coping with the high notes, while those in the lower register would be entrusted to the fourth. Once valve-horns became generally available it became the normal custom to write all horn-parts in F, transposed a fifth higher than the actual sound. There would appear to be no particular reason for this except that it tends to keep the part comfortably within one stave, minimizing the use of leger lines. The instrument has a wide compass:

However, the extreme notes are insecure and rarely used without adequate cover from the rest of the orchestra. Such at least was the case until about 1960, when the invention of a 'double' horn made the player's task considerably less hazardous. Effectively two instruments in one, it can be converted into a horn in high B flat at the touch of a switch, making the whole upper range more accessible and less prone to disaster.

An enquiring mind may ask why it is that if in both woodwind and strings the highest instruments are placed at the top of their group in the score, the horns are not found *below* the trumpets. The reason is practical; as often as not the horns act as auxiliaries to the woodwind, frequently being called upon to blend with clarinets or bassoons. Such a blend is easier for the conductor to spot if horns and wind lie close together on the page. The horns are often used to fill-in or to sustain harmony, but when they are employed in a solo capacity or as a four-part group they can be highly effective. The slow movement of Tchaikovsky's Fifth Symphony is a classic instance of the 'romantic' horn tune, while Beethoven's use of three horns in the Trio from the 'Eroica' symphony shows how effectively the old-time natural horns could be used. As for the notorious horn solo featured in Strauss's *Till Eulenspiegel*, it brilliantly combines the best attributes of the modern valve-horn with the character of the original natural horn.

The **Trumpet**, the harbinger of war, has an ancient history as we have seen. Its evolution in Western music is not dissimilar to the horn's in that it too is limited to the notes of the harmonic series, it too acquired valves (or to be more accurate pistons) to enlarge its range. No instrument suffered a sadder decline in the mid-eighteenth century nor underwent a more glorious rebirth a hundred or so years later. There is, too, a certain irony in the fact that it was self-taught jazz players who began once again to open up its extreme upper register, re-discovering the technical secrets of Bach's age. In one of the first commissioned scores I ever wrote for the BBC (in about 1945) I included a top D in the trumpet part. I was told scornfully by the player that the note didn't exist; when I said that I had heard jazz players go up to a top F, he said, 'But look what a filthy row they make!'

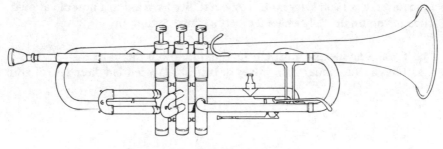

Trumpet

As with the horn, it was necessary at first for players to use crooks if they wished to change key; the same permanent C major notation was also used with a preliminary instruction 'Trumpets in A' or 'Trumpets in D'. (Trumpets in Bach's time were normally pitched in D so that choruses of jubilation or triumph were almost invariably in that key.) But just as the horn tended ultimately to settle for F as the most convenient permanent tuning, so the trumpet became by general consent an instrument in B flat, although many composers nowadays write their trumpet-parts in C, that is to say at the

45

actual pitch. Even so, other variants have survived. Sibelius, for example, showed a marked preference for the larger trumpet in F. It is one of the most misleading of instruments to the conductor's *eye* since it transposes in such a way that the part is written a fourth lower than it sounds. Many a trumpet-passage in a Sibelius symphony looks as if it is lying in a rather boring register when in fact it is sailing high above the rest of the brass.

It is only natural to associate trumpets with pageantry or war, but they are capable of expressive and lyrical playing, as composers such as Aaron Copland have amply demonstrated (*Quiet City, Billy the Kid*). A number of different mutes are available to distort or disguise its natural tone, but these can be used to excess. As to its range, much depends on the skill of the performer; the text-books normally give a compass of some two and a half octaves:

By modern standards this is very conservative at the upper end.

Other members of the trumpet-family include the **Cornet**, much used by Berlioz but nowadays banished more or less permanently to brass and silver bands where it can demonstrate its remarkable agility to good purpose; there is also the **Flügelhorn**, a wonderfully mellow-toned instrument with a similar compass to the cornet but a more full-bodied sound. (Strictly speaking it should be classified as a soprano sax-horn, a subtlety of nomenclature I would prefer not to have to expound.) Much used in jazz and in brass bands, it acquired a certain symphonic respectability by making a notable appearance in the finale of Michael Tippett's Third Symphony.

The **Trombone** has the most unusual feature of all the brass instruments in that it has a slide rather than valves or pistons. Descended directly from the

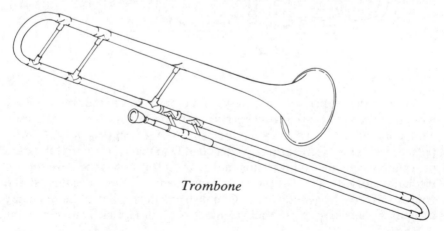

Trombone

Sackbut of medieval times, it shares with other brass instruments the limitations of the harmonic series. In what is known as the First Position, the slide being closed right up so that the tube is at its shortest, the player can produce the following notes purely by lip adjustment:

By letting the slide out to the Second Position he can produce a similar sequence a semitone lower; the Third Position will give a series a tone lower (starting on A flat) and so on, there being seven positions in all.

This would give an effective chromatic compass from low E to high B flat.

(Note the use of the 'tenor' clef in which the second line from the top indicates 'middle' C.) As with the horn, recent innovations have considerably widened the scope of the instrument, as we shall see when we come to the larger member of the family, the bass trombone.

It should be explained that the trombones are normally grouped as a trio of two tenors and one bass, since their function is often to supply a well-blended foundation to the brass harmony. For a long period the **Bass Trombone** did not have a substantially deeper range than the Tenor, presumably owing to the limited length of the human arm. In fact a small rod was needed to enable the player to use the full extension of the instrument, sounding the C sharp below the bass stave. This somewhat makeshift device has now been supplanted by an ingenious mechanism which literally at the press of a button puts the instrument into F, thereby widening the downward compass considerably, taking it down to a low B flat and even beyond. Tenor and bass trombone now only differ in the size of bore, the bass being slightly larger so as to improve the quality of tone in the lowest register.

The blend between tenor and bass trombones is particularly satisfying, whether in *fortissimo* passages or when muted. Allowed to show their full power, they can dominate an orchestra of a hundred players with ease. There can be few more thrilling sounds than the trombones in full cry in the Prelude to Act III of Wagner's *Lohengrin*; yet they can be wonderfully effective in quiet chorale-like passages, witness the solemn E major section in the finale of Brahms's Fourth Symphony. A notable example of daring in orchestration occurs in the slow movement of the Elgar violin concerto, where the composer elects to accompany the solo violin with sumptuous harmonies from the trombones. On paper it looks like a wild miscalculation, but in performance it comes off to marvellous effect.

Mention should also be made of the **Alto Trombone** in E flat which, having fallen into disuse during the nineteenth century, has made something of a come-back in recent years, both in jazz and in orchestral music. As would be expected, it opens up a higher register which can be exploited most effectively, as Britten showed in his church parable *The Burning Fiery Furnace*.

The true bass to the orchestral brass family is the **Tuba**. Like the trombones, it is a non-transposing instrument but, like the trumpets, is equipped with piston-type valves of which it has four. Surprisingly nimble for its size, it is an instrument with a relatively short orchestral life, dating from the second half of the nineteenth century. Tubas come in several sizes with a coiled tube-length varying from nine to sixteen feet. The smaller size is usually known as a euphonium, being very popular in brass and silver bands as an approximate equivalent to a viola section. The most common tuba in orchestral works is the Tuba in F, with a compass of three octaves.

Tuba

It was primarily Wagner who was responsible for the development of the tuba family; dissatisfied with the obsolescent serpent and ophicleide, he sought what might be described as the brass equivalent to a male voice choir. The original Wagner tubas were little more than modified French horns, but in due course the instrument we now recognize came into being. Its slightly woolly tone makes it a less than ideal match for the trombones, yet there is no doubt that it adds effectiveness to the bass-line; nobody who has heard the overture to Wagner's *Die Meistersinger* will readily forget the final convergence of themes in which the bass part stands out with the greatest clarity thanks to the tuba. Nor, in very different guise, can one fail to recognize its portrayal of the tormented bear in Stravinsky's *Petrushka*, or the eerie fog-horn in the closing scene of Britten's *Peter Grimes*.

Here, then, is the brass section of the modern symphony orchestra, considerably enlarged from the two trumpets and two horns of Haydn's time. Nowadays three trumpets, four or five horns, three trombones and tuba are the standard requirement. The most substantial works of Mahler, Bruckner, Schoenberg or Stockhausen may demand considerably larger resources, whether to impress by sheer weight of sound (as for that matter did Berlioz in his Requiem), or to exalt us with the earthly depiction of angelic trumpets. While it is true that an excess of brass may court vulgarity, there is no denying the splendour of its sounds. Can anyone listen to the fugal brass fanfares in the Bartók *Concerto for Orchestra* without a quickening of the pulse or fail to respond to the impact of the brass bands that Walton introduced into *Belshazzar's Feast*? Yet even that heady excitement can be made more feverish by the addition of percussion.

The Percussion

Although percussion instruments date back to the most primitive period of man, since when their existence in one form or other has continued in an unbroken line, they remained for centuries the least developed section of the orchestra. During the Middle Ages all popular music would have had its rhythmic pulse emphasized by some type of drum, usually the small tabor or tabret, but the timbrel (a precursor of our Tambourine), castanets or clappers and even a triangle with jingling rings were all in common use. Small cymbals or crotales can be traced back to ancient Egypt, gongs to China, while the **Kettledrums** arrived in Europe with the Saracens in the thirteenth century. Initially these drums (known as 'nakers') were quite small and shallow but two centuries later much larger instruments appeared in the Ottoman Empire, played by drummers mounted on camel or horseback. Such drums would have been pitched to two different notes by the simple device of making one larger than the other. By the seventeenth century European instrument-makers had invented a method of tuning individual kettledrums by a system of screws that could tighten or slacken the vellum

49

head, thus raising or lowering the pitch. The drums called for by Bach, Handel and their contemporaries were simply imported cavalry drums played with hard wooden beaters that permitted little subtlety of tone. They were almost invariably tuned to the tonic and dominant notes of the required key (usually D or C to suit the trumpets), nor was the pitch changed during a movement. Over the years improvements were gradually introduced, especially in the provision of a variety of heads on the drumsticks so as to offer more subtleties of tone. Berlioz, a daring innovator in his use of percussion, cites three different types of drumstick currently in use, those with wooden ends – 'scarcely good for anything but to strike a violent blow' – those with wooden ends covered with leather – 'less hard, but very dry nevertheless' – and those with ends of sponge which he regarded as greatly superior, regretting that their use was not more frequent. The timpanist in a modern symphony orchestra will have a wide range of sticks of varying hardness, the heads being made of balsa wood or cork with a covering of felt.

It is an unwritten law of orchestral decorum that one refers to the timpanist neither as a drummer nor even as a member of the percussion group. Playing the kettledrums (timpani) is a highly skilled art requiring the supplest of wrists and keenest of ears. The player often has to tune his instruments virtually inaudibly while the full blast of orchestral tone is ringing round his head. Formerly such changes had to be done by hand-operated screws, eight in number, each of which had to be adjusted in turn to

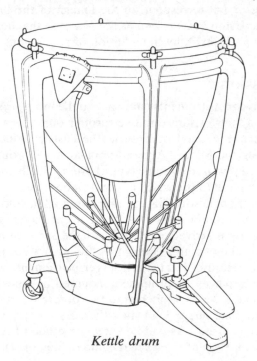

Kettle drum

hair's breadth accuracy. The modern instruments give the player an easier time, the change of pitch being effected with a pedal (not unlike the clutch pedal in a car) which even has the various gradations of pitch marked on a scale.

While Mozart and Haydn used kettledrums to good effect in their orchestral works, it was Beethoven who gave the timpani a more imaginative and musical part to play. The quiet drum-taps at the start of his violin concerto do not simply mark the time; they are an integral part of the thematic material of the movement. The long passage for timpani that leads into the finale of the Fifth Symphony creates a spellbinding effect, while the timpanist's duet with the solo pianist towards the end of the 'Emperor' Concerto is a stroke of true genius. It was Beethoven, too, who experimented with the tuning of the timpani, breaking away from the convention of tonic-dominant; for example, in both the Eighth and Ninth Symphonies he tunes his timpani an octave apart – a wasteful duplication one would imagine, until one hears how effective it is.

With the timpani thus liberated from the most pedestrian of roles, it was Berlioz who made the most inventive use of them. In the *Symphonie Fantastique* he uses four timpani played by four musicians to produce a simulation of thunder:

Elsewhere he spells out a four-note melody on timpani, while in the Requiem he indulges himself in a glorious welter of sound with ten timpanists playing sixteen timpani between them, using two extra 'long drums' lest he should be accused of skimping his resources.

Each kettledrum can be tuned to any note within a range of approximately a fifth; it is for this reason that the timpanist in the modern orchestra will be seen to employ three or more instruments so as to be able to cover a full octave. Even in the nineteenth century, composers would often call for three timpani whose respective ranges (according to size) would be

Equipped with three such instruments, the player would have the advantage of being able to tune them in advance to a number of notes, thus eliminating the awkward problem of re-tuning during a movement.

The timpani are sometimes muted or 'damped' by laying a soft cloth on the head, a technique that can also be employed with the side drum.

The **Side Drum** or military drum is made of metal with a parchment (sheep-skin) head on each side. Across the lower head are stretched a small number of catgut or wire cords known as 'snares'. (It is sometimes referred to as a 'snare-drum'.) When the drummer strikes the upper head of the instrument the sound-waves pass through the hollow shell and set up a sympathetic vibration in the lower skin which is amplified by the contact with the snares. If the snares are slackened off so as to lose contact, the tone of the instrument is deadened and lacks its characteristic crackle. Played with a pair of wooden sticks, the instrument is ideal for pointing crisp rhythms or for sustained rolls. Whereas a roll on the timpani is played with alternate hands, the side-drum roll is played as a 'double' beat, two strikes with the left stick, two with the right and so on. This is known as 'Dad-dy—Mam-my', not to be confused with a 'Paradiddle', which is a special method of playing repeated notes so that the accented beats fall on alternate sticks, for example,

or { L R L L   R L R R
   { R L R R   L R L L

but NOT   L R L R   L R L R

    The tautness of the side-drum head is one of its most essential features since in rapid passages the sticks literally bounce off the skin. (Nowadays plastic heads are frequently used both on timpani and side drums though many players still have an affection for sheepskin or calfskin.) Unlike the timpani the side drum has no determined pitch; it is therefore a good mixer, the tonality of the music being irrelevant.

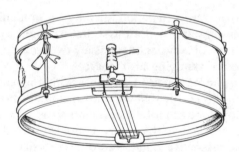

Side drum

The **Tenor Drum** might be described as the side drum's big brother. It is more familiar in military bands than in symphony orchestras, but its some-what hollow tone, caused by its deeper shell, can be very effective. It is generally played with hard felt sticks whose heads are approximately the size of a ping-pong ball. The skins are tautened by a system of cords that join them together.

Tenor drum

The **Bass Drum** is sometimes made with only one head, sometimes with two. The single-headed instrument is known as a Gong Drum. Owing to the size of the skin, a minimum of twenty-eight inches, it is impossible to do an effective fast roll on the instrument because the vibrations begin to overlap.

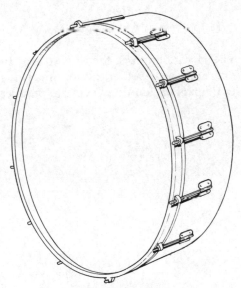

Bass drum

Even so, it can produce a wonderfully ominous rumble if required, while individual strokes *fortissimo* can sound like cannon shots. Like the side-drum, it has no definite pitch although, if subtly blended with a quiet *tremolando* from the double-basses, it can deceive the listener, giving the illusion that it is playing the same note.

The **Tambourine** might be said to belong to the drum family since it too has a circular vellum head and is struck with the fingers or even on occasion with side-drum sticks. Inserted into its side wall are small metal plates that give a pleasing jangle. They may be shaken or rolled with the thumb. Its musical potential tends to be limited by its strong association with certain types of nationalistic music.

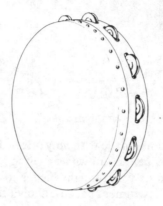

Tambourine

The **Cymbals** come in various sizes, the largest ones being capable of an extremely wide range of tone, whether clashed openly to provide a climax or struck gently with timpani or side-drum sticks to produce a sinister metallic

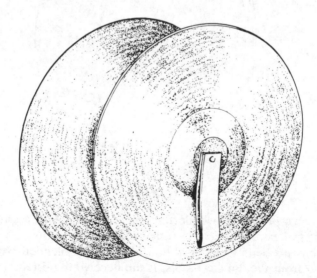

Cymbals

rustle. Small cymbals such as are to be found in children's percussion bands are little more effective than saucepan-lids, but the ancient tiny cymbals known as 'crotales' have an enchanting bell-like tone, beautifully exploited by Berlioz in the Queen Mab scherzo from his *Romeo and Juliet* symphony.

The **Gong** or **Tam-Tam** comes from the Far East; it has an awe-inspiring ability to approach the threshold of pain in crescendo, the vibrations it sets up seeming to be self-reproductive. It can do considerably more than lend a touch of Oriental colour, as Tchaikovsky demonstrated to such wonderful effect in the closing movement of his Sixth Symphony; more chilling than any conventional bell, it strikes a truly funereal note.

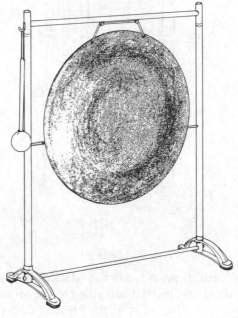

Gong (Tam-tam)

The **Tubular Bells** or **Chimes** consist of a set of eighteen hollow metal tubes suspended in a frame so that each may vibrate freely. A damping mechanism is provided to check the sound if required, although the bells are usually at their most effective when the tone is allowed to die away naturally. A small mallet covered with rawhide is normally used as a beater, though composers have been known to ask for a metal striker. The available compass is approximately one and a half octaves:

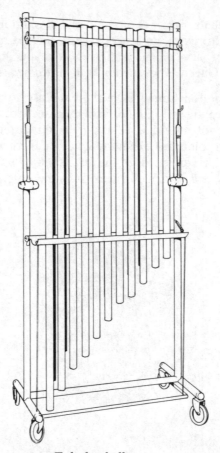

Tubular bells

A miniature set of 'bells' is provided in the **Glockenspiel**; it consists not of bells but of tuned metal bars laid flat according to the disposition of a piano keyboard. Originally a toy imitation of the Flemish Church Carillons, the version required by Mozart in *The Magic Flute* or by Handel in *Saul* did have a keyboard action. (Such an instrument was even specified in Dukas's *Sorcerer's Apprentice* though modern percussion players seldom use it, examples being extremely rare.) An instrument that has a touch of fairy enchantment about it when played quietly, it can also make its presence felt surprisingly well even against a powerful tutti. There are two sizes available, one with twenty-seven notes, the other with thirty-seven. The more common instrument has the compass

the notes being written two octaves below their actual pitch.

56

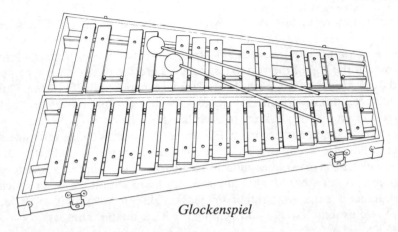

Glockenspiel

Unlike the metal Glockenspiel, the **Xylophone** consists of wooden bars whose tone-quality is assisted by resonators. The lay-out is again based on the piano keyboard but the tone cannot be sustained except by a rapid reiteration of the note. Ideal for brittle rhythmic figuration, it can be used in passages of great agility providing that they are written with a proper regard for the technique of playing with two beaters. The compass varies, some instruments being larger than other; three and a half octaves is normal, from

to high C.

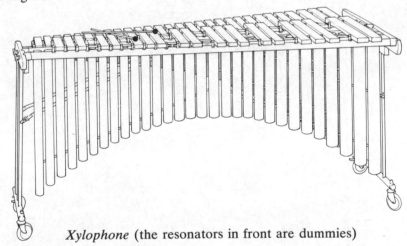

Xylophone (the resonators in front are dummies)

All such instruments are clearly descended from the tuned percussion of the Gamelan orchestras of Indonesia. The European manufacturers have simply incorporated refinements made practical by modern technology. Thus the **Marimba** is a deeper, more mellow-sounding xylophone capable of a

57

somewhat more sustained tone, while the **Vibraphone** might be described as a deep-voiced glockenspiel with the added capability of playing vibrato. This is accomplished by a small electric motor that causes butterfly fans to revolve at the top of the resonating tubes. Like the piano it has a damping pedal since the tone can be prolonged for an exceptionally long time. Played without the motor-driven fans, its tone is considerably deadened. Skilled players often use two beaters in each hand, playing four-note chords with remarkable speed and accuracy. Extremely popular as a solo instrument in jazz, it has also found a place in the modern symphony orchestra and is especially useful in evoking underwater images or the empty and mysterious regions of outer space. It should not be confused with the **Celesta** which in appearance resembles a rather unpleasant design of minipiano. It has a keyboard exactly like a piano's, though with a smaller compass.

sounding an octave higher.

As with the glockenspiel the tone is produced from metal bars each with an accurately tuned wooden resonator. The tone is bell-like but nicely rounded. By chance Tchaikovsky heard it in the inventor's workshop in

Celesta

Paris; bewitched by its musical-box tones, he immortalized it with the *Dance of the Sugar-Plum Fairy*.

Strictly speaking, the celesta is not a percussion instrument in orchestral players' terms since it will be played by an 'extra' brought in for the occasion rather than one of the official percussionists.

To catalogue all the instruments that do come into the category of percussion is a huge and (for the audience) an unnecessary task. There are many varieties of drum, temple blocks, wooden blocks, bongos, whistles, anvils, triangles of different sizes, suspended cymbals, South American exotica such as the claves (two cane sticks) or the guiro (a notched gourd with a scraper), maracas – even in two notorious instances chains and a immense hammer. No section of the orchestra has undergone such an enormous development, much of it during the twentieth century. When Mozart wished to use the largest available percussion resources in his opera *Die Entführung aus dem Serail* he asked for timpani, triangle, cymbals and bass drum – precisely what Beethoven used in the finale of the Ninth Symphony. Haydn used the same in his Symphony No. 100, the *Military*, to such effect that ladies in the audience were near to fainting. One stroke on the gong in the Cherubini Requiem caused a scandalized reaction amongst the critics. No longer does the percussion section consist of 'thump-and-count' men; rather are they the most versatile performers in the orchestra. They need quickness of wit – not to mention nimbleness of foot – and their resourcefulness in meeting ever new demands is a composer's delight. (I once scored a short TV ballet for thirty-two percussion instruments played by two players.) A top percussion player will spend many thousands of pounds on instruments even though some major items may belong to the orchestra in which he plays. Having spent perhaps undue space on this relatively new aspect of orchestral music, it is now time to turn to the true foundation of orchestral sound.

The Strings

The **Violin**. The principle of stretching strings over a hollow resonating box to improve the tone quality was discovered at least two thousand years ago, although the idea of causing the strings to vibrate by rubbing them with a bow was a later development. During the Middle Ages an ingenious but now unknown inventor devised an instrument with three strings drawn tightly over a sound-box, so arranged as to form an arc. Beneath this arc was a wooden wheel, leather lined and cranked by a handle. As the wheel rotated it rubbed against the strings causing all three to sound at once; meanwhile a little 'bridge' across the strings could be moved back and forth so as to change the pitch. The result was a series of three-note chords moving in parallel; the tone can only have been unpleasant, but was presumably music to the performers' ears. (Two players were required.) Called the Organistrum, it duly evolved into the Hurdy-gurdy or Vielle. Its relationship to the violin may indeed seem to be remote but it was partly through such unlikely ancestry that the instrument came into being.

Centuries earlier a bowed lute had appeared in Southern Asia; it was probably introduced into Europe by the Arabs in a somewhat pear-shaped form, and in its early days it was called a Rebec. During the thirteenth century modifications to its shape continued to be made, and it was then that it acquired the more familiar sounding name of Fidel or, as it came to be spelt, Fiddle. In the course of some two centuries a number of improvements were made, including an extension to the length of the neck and a sophisticated attempt to improve the quality of tone by the provision of 'sympathetic' strings which were not actually played but which acted as a primitive amplifier. It was this line of development that led to the whole family of Viols, instruments that should not be regarded as predecessors of the violin but rather as a different evolutionary branch of the string group.

Surprisingly, considering how poorly it was to be regarded in the seventeenth and eighteenth centuries, the viola was the first of the modern string instruments to emerge, presumably because its range was most apt for the accompaniment of male voices in priestly song. The word Violin, or more properly Violino, simply means a small Viola; the word Violone was applied to the early double-bass, a Violoncello being a 'small double bass'.

The first true violin appeared around 1550, its essential differences from any of its precursors being that it had four strings tuned a fifth apart from each other, that it was played on the arm with a bow, that its fingerboard or neck had no frets to guide the player's fingers and that its lowest note was the G below middle C. Almost exactly a hundred years later Antonio Stradivari was born (1644–1737). Most famous of violin-makers though he is, he was greatly indebted to the Amati family, to whom he was apprenticed and who had been making fine instruments for nearly a century. Also apprenticed to Nicolo Amati was Andrea Guarneri, founding father of another great line of violin-makers; his grandson, Giuseppe Guarneri (1698–1744) was perhaps the only true rival to Stradivari, his instruments being notable for their sonority.

It is a unique phenomenon in the musical world that a very considerable number of instruments made approximately two and a half centuries ago should not only still be in use but should never have been surpassed in quality. That they should all have come from two relatively obscure towns in Italy, Cremona and Brescia, only adds to the mystery. Even modern scientific research has been unable to trace the elusive elements that give these instruments their unparalleled qualities; we can only be grateful that so many have survived to set a standard by which every subsequent instrument must be judged. All the same it must be remembered that the 'Strad' of today is not as its maker left it. During the latter part of the eighteenth century a number of modifications became necessary to meet the new demands of composers. In the search for bigger tone, greater brilliance and an extension of the range, the sound post that joins the 'back' and the 'belly' of the instrument was strengthened, the neck was lengthened, the finger-board beneath the strings was extended, the bridge raised and, in time, a chin-rest was added. Furthermore the techniques of playing were greatly developed, most remarkably by the legendary Niccolò Paganini (1782–1840). It is worth mentioning that Paganini by preference played a violin by Giuseppi Guarneri. (Stradivarius and Guarnerius are Latinized versions of the makers' names, used rather as trade-marks.)

Although at first regarded with the habitual distaste and suspicion that innovations elicit, the violin was soon to become the dominating string instrument, a position from which it shows no sign of being dislodged. Its greatest advantage over its rivals was its subtlety of nuance and, in the right hands, its trueness of intonation. Moreover the blend of violins, violas, cellos and basses was unsurpassed. Here, then, was a corporate body of matched sound that was needed as the foundation of that concept we know as the orchestra.

Violin

Although it is not within the province of this book to be a string tutor, the basic principles of string playing should perhaps be explained. In effect the violinist plays an ascending scale by shortening the string with the pressure of a finger. Since he has only four fingers, the thumb being used as a support for the neck of the instrument, he has either to cross over to another string to continue the scale or to shift the position of his hand, climbing crabwise towards the bridge across which the strings are drawn. These shifts have to be practised rigorously until absolute precision can be acquired. Seven positions are the norm for an advanced player, but for extremely high notes still further positions can be contrived, though the fingers will now be so close together as almost to overlap. Whereas on the instruments so far discussed the actual distance between notes is dictated by keys or by the player's lip-tension, string players have to make continuous fine adjustments, the difference between tones and semitones varying with each change of hand position. This is most easily observed on the cello where the first steps in the climb up a string involve a considerable gap between the fingers (uncomfortable for a small hand) which visibly diminishes the higher the player goes in the scale; at the extreme upper register the fingers will be touching.

A great number of different effects are available to the skilled player, two-, three- and four-note chords, a variety of bowings from the most seamless legato to a sparkling staccato caused by literally bouncing the bow off the string, tremolando, pizzicato (plucking the string with the finger), even left-hand pizzicato – though this is seldom called for in orchestral work. In addition it is possible to exploit aspects of that same harmonic series we have already come across in our study of the brass (see page 42). If a violin string is lightly touched at its halfway point, it will sound the note an octave higher than would the unstopped string. The sound is thin and ethereal. Other harmonics may be produced by touching the string at various fractional lengths, $\frac{1}{3}$, $\frac{2}{3}$, $\frac{1}{4}$, $\frac{3}{4}$, $\frac{1}{5}$, $\frac{3}{5}$, $\frac{1}{6}$ and $\frac{5}{6}$. All these are known as Natural Harmonics and provide alternative ways of producing the second to the sixth overtones from the fundamental string. But there is also a way of producing Artificial Harmonics; the first finger is placed firmly on the string to provide a new fundamental; the player then touches the string very lightly with his little finger a perfect fourth higher. The sound that ensues will be pitched two octaves higher than the note he is pressing firmly with his first finger. For example, by placing his first finger on the note B (obtainable only on the G string)

and then very lightly touching the E above

 ,

the actual sound produced will be this B.

It only needs a moment's thought to see that the use of this technique not only provides an interestingly different, if rather ghostly, tone-colour but that it also extends the upper range of the instrument considerably. All string instruments can produce harmonics, and the effect is frequently exploited in the more colourful scores. Harmonic glissandi, sliding the finger superficially up and down the string, are used by Stravinsky in *The Firebird* and by Britten in *Les Illuminations*. Natural harmonics are indicated by placing a small circle above the written note,

 ,

while artificial harmonics are written with a diamond-shaped head a fourth above the firmly stopped note.

The tuning of violin, viola and cello is in fifths:

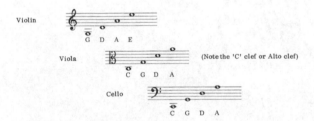

The double bass, whose great length of string demands very wide spacing of the fingers in the early stages of a scale, is, consequently, tuned in fourths.

In modern orchestras there will always be some players with the added luxury of a fifth string going down to the low C, thus being able to duplicate the whole range of the cello. There is also the C-string attachment, a mechanical device that re-tunes the lowest string down to C if required.

As has already been suggested, the principles of string playing apply to all four instruments, but for the sake of completeness one should devote some space to the deeper-voiced members.

The **Viola**. While, as has already been implied, there was a period when the viola section was technically the weakest of the strings, during the nineteenth century composers began to make increasing demands on the players until, in scores of the last hundred years or so, there is little variation in difficulty between the violin and viola parts. It is true, though, that many viola players begin their instrumental experience on the violin; the instrument is cumbersome to handle for a child and half or three-quarter size violas are hard to obtain. It is worth mentioning that many great violinists

Viola

love to play the viola, relishing the extra richness of tone from the lower strings. However, to sustain an equal mastery of both instruments at one and the same time is a severe challenge since, clearly, the precise placing of the fingers (so essential for true intonation) is marginally different. Owing to the size of the viola its normal working compass is limited to about three octaves; if the player attempts to go above the Fifth position (see p. 62) the 'shoulder' of the instrument will block his hand. Being essentially a middle register instrument, it is inevitable that viola players are seldom allowed top-line melodies; either they play in unison with the violins (or cellos) or else they are given figurations based on harmony to fill in the texture.

Moments of glory may be few and far between but perhaps they are appreciated all the more for that. It is said that both Haydn and Mozart preferred to play the viola in string quartets since there they were in the heart of the harmony.

Bowing and fingering techniques are identical in violin and viola playing but the part will mostly be written in the 'C' or Alto clef except when it rises into the upper register.

The **Violoncello**, or cello as it is more commonly known, is supported on the floor by a retractable metal spike and balanced between the player's knees. Owing to its substantially greater length of string, the intervals of tones or semitones demand a wider extension between the fingers than is required on the violin or viola. Consequently the cellist must become very proficient in shifting the position of his left hand since the interval between the index

Violoncello

finger and the little finger is only a major third. Although little is known about him, it was an eighteenth-century player called (suitably enough) Franciscello who devised the solution to the problems of this manual limitation. When a violinist shifts his left hand position he still maintains contact with the neck of the instrument with his thumb. With the greater length of the cello this becomes impossible as the higher notes are reached. Franciscello therefore taught himself to use his thumb as a sort of movable gauge which would anchor the hand in place. When we realize that every note above this D

requires a shift of position the need for some such device becomes apparent. Thumb positions, as they are called, become necessary from this B (on the A string)

but are just as likely to be used on the lower strings by cellists, fingering being a matter for individual preference. Other cellists, notably the Duport brothers in France, developed Franciscello's technique, also copying his revolutionary idea of holding the bow with the palm facing downwards instead of the cupped hand position favoured by viola da gamba players. Not only did the use of the new thumb positions open up what might be described as the uncharted areas of the instrument; it also brought an aesthetic advantage by enabling the player to stay on one string for a greater proportion of any one melodic line. (Even more than with the violin there is a marked difference of quality between the various strings and constant changes of tone-colour can be disturbing.) In certain ways the technique of fingering on the cello is more straightforward than that of the violin in spite of its apparent limitations; in a diatonic scale the cellist has the choice of four fingers to play three notes, whereas the violinist has a ratio of four to four; in a chromatic scale the cellist's fingers will have to cope with five semitones before a shift, the violinist with six or more.

Cellists must be familiar with three clefs, the bass and treble which are in common use, but also the tenor:

≗ middle C

An appalling and illogical eccentricity of notation crept in during the nineteenth century which may have baffled many an amateur score-reader. Examples are frequently found in works such as the Beethoven quartets, in which once the cello part rises into the treble clef it is written an octave higher than the sound required. As an instance of the sheer idiocy of some aspects of musical notation it could hardly be excelled; happily it is no longer employed. However, it does provide a useful link to lead us to the **Double Bass** or **Contrabass**, whose music is invariably written an octave higher than the intended sound. I say 'invariably' with the slight but significant reservation that during the seventeenth and eighteenth centuries, and indeed well into Beethoven's time, the bass was usually a three-string instrument so tuned that the lowest note was the A or G below the bass stave, according to the player's preference. (Four-, even five- or six-string instruments were made, but the three-string bass prevailed for the better part of a century.) Since composers of that era seldom bothered to write a separate bass part, the player used his discretion and initiative whenever the cello part (which he was duplicating) wandered beyond his range or ability. For example, if the cello was required to play some such sequence as this:

Double Bass

the bass section of the orchestra, unable to go below A, would automatically modify the passage without instruction to do so, perhaps on these lines:

The practice of simplifying or 'editing' quicker passages was quite common among bass-players, and it is worth remarking that at the first performance of Beethoven's Choral Symphony the recitative passages that make such a dramatic effect near the start of the last movement were played as a *solo* by the great double bass virtuoso Dragonetti, very probably because the combined bass section found them too hazardous.

The system of tuning the bass in fourths instead of the fifths employed in the other strings is dictated by the considerably wider intervals between notes, for bass-players seldom use two adjacent fingers in scale passages except when playing in the highest register. The bow is rather short in proportion to the size of the instrument; its hair is black and coarser in texture than a cello bow. Furthermore there are two distinct types of bow: most commonly used in this country is the so-called French bow, not unlike that of a cello though heavier, thicker and more curved. It is held palm downwards, cello-style. In Europe there is a preference for the 'Simandl' bow, named after a noted Austrian bass-player of the nineteenth century; it is held with the palm cupped beneath it, thus perpetuating the mode of playing that originated with the viols.

With so long a string the instrument takes a fractional time to 'speak'; nevertheless the agility of the modern orchestral players is astonishing and they seem to take a delight in showing that the cellos cannot outpace them. Although not often entrusted with passages entirely to themselves, the basses are a very essential foundation for the string ensemble; even a single player makes a noticable difference to a small orchestra. Verdi used the bass section to wonderful effect at the start of the closing scene of *Otello*, a passage of notorious difficulty. In a very different category, jazz bassists have developed extraordinarily rapid pizzicato techniques; indeed, the pizzicato tones of the double bass are one of the most effective sounds in the orchestra.

The **Harp** was not in general use as an orchestral instrument until the nineteenth century despite its great antiquity in various forms. All the early versions of the harp suffered from a serious limitation which can be briefly summed up in the phrase 'one string, one note'. Whereas such plucked instruments as the lute or guitar could, by using the fingers of the left hand, provide a full chromatic compass, the harp was in effect a string instrument with nothing but 'open' strings. A moment's thought tells us that the number of such strings that can be incorporated is limited by the length of the human

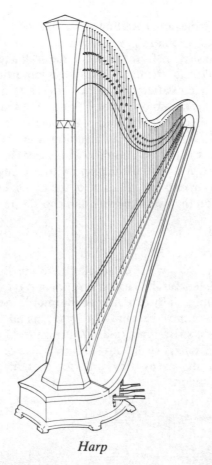

Harp

arm. Imagine standing at one side of a grand piano looking at the strings in the interior; one could reach approximately half way across the instrument. It is not surprising, then, that the harp has only forty-seven strings compared to the piano's eighty-eight keys. (The piano has a substantially larger number of actual 'strings' since many of its notes are triple-strung and some double-strung; only the bottom register has a single string to each note, and those so massive that they could scarcely be plucked by the human finger.)

Improvements to the harp designed to overcome this shortcoming date initially from 1720, but it was not until the first decade of the nineteenth century that a satisfactory solution was found – by the French instrument-maker Sébastien Erard (1752–1831), who invented what is known as the Double Action Harp. By the application of seven pedals, one for each note of the diatonic scale, he made it possible for the player to cause each string to play three notes, the 'flat', the 'natural' and the 'sharp'. He constructed his harp so that it was tuned in the theoretical key of C flat; a pianist would call it B major but the reason for Erard's seemingly perverse notation soon becomes clear. In the initial setting or tuning of the harp, all notes are flattened. The depression of the pedal connected to *all* the C strings would, in its first notch, raise them from C flat to C natural; a further depression to a second notch would raise them to C sharp. It is important to understand that each of the seven pedals affects all of the strings associated with it by name, *all* the Gs, *all* the Ds and so on. Since E flat and D sharp are (near enough) the same note enharmonically, and since such enharmonic duplications abound in music, it is possible by an ingenious use of the pedals to produce an effect unique to the harp, a glissando with spaces in it. Any child can play a glissando on the white notes of the piano with one finger; a harpist can play a glissando which appears to omit some of the notes. Let us suppose that we want a glissando on that well-known crisis chord, the diminished seventh.

The chromatic notes we need to eliminate are B natural, C sharp, D natural, E natural, F natural, G natural, A flat and B flat – quite a tall order. The harpist goes about it by exploiting enharmonic identities. By tuning all 'B' strings to B sharp they 'become' Cs. By tuning all 'D' strings to D sharp they 'become' E flats. By tuning all 'G' strings to G flat they 'become' F sharps. The C, E, F and A strings are already bespoke in the desired chord. Pass a hand over the harp-strings in slow motion and you will hear a sequence of duplications

At speed the ear fails to pick these up and we imagine we are hearing a rapid arpeggio:

Providing that each note in the alphabetical series A—G can be accounted for enharmonically by treating it as 'flat', 'natural' or 'sharp', composers can devise a number of interesting note-sequences that can be treated in this way. The harpist is given due warning to pre-set the pedals by letter notation (A natural, B flat, C natural, D flat, E sharp, F natural, G flat) or by the indication of any alterations that need to be made from a previous setting (Muta [i.e. change] A flat—natural, B sharp—flat, E flat—sharp).

70

The sound produced by the setting shown above would be this, assuming the composer wished to start the arpeggio-glissando on B flat.

To write out all the notes in such a passage is unnecessarily laborious; the conventional short-cuts are either to write the first seven notes ascending followed by a diagonal line to the required top note or simply to indicate the first and last notes of the glissando and connect them.

Alternatively the first four notes of the glissando may be indicated at the 'point of departure', the last three at the 'point of arrival'.

Fascinating though the sound may be, glissandi are only a small aspect of harp-playing. Chords, arpeggios, accompanying figures, even solo melodies with built-in accompaniments are all to be found in orchestral harp parts. In harp solos the player is sometimes even required to tap the body of the instrument in a simulated drum effect. An especially subtle and beautiful sound is obtained by the use of harmonics; the player 'stops' the string at its half-way point with the lower edge of the palm, plucking the upper part of the string with the fingers. The sound is ethereal and bell-like, the note sounded being an octave higher than that normally given by the string.

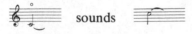 sounds

The small circle above the written note indicates that a harmonic is required.

For some reason that harpists have never satisfactorily explained to me, the little finger is never used in harp-playing; the largest chord that can be played therefore consists of eight notes, four to each hand. Because of the harp's very individual system, the most convenient notation for a chord often looks very strange to a pianist's eye. A harpist would not be the least bit perturbed to find the chord of C minor written thus:

71

Full Score

* The placing of the harp parts is optional;
they are often to be found between the
percussion and strings.

To a pianist with conventional conceptions of harmony such an aberration seems pointless, but if it saves a harpist a couple of pedal-changes in the next bar, it would be perfectly sensible.

The use of two harps in an orchestra enables the composer to indulge in changes of harmony too swift for a single player to cope with; the two players will seldom duplicate each other but rather will complement each other's harmonic resources. Although Beethoven wrote a harp part in his ballet-music to *Prometheus*, presumably because there was a resident harpist in the theatre orchestra, he never used one in his symphonies. It was Berlioz who first introduced the harp into a large-scale symphonic work, in the Ballroom Scene from the *Symphonie Fantastique*. Perhaps because so many of the best harps were French-made, French composers seem to have had an especial sympathy and affection for the instrument; nobody has written more exquisitely for it than Ravel and Debussy. Pitted against a full orchestra the harp will be virtually inaudible; essentially it should be reserved for subtle and delicate effects although, if allowed to behave as a solo instrument, it can make a brave enough showing. For instance, the cadenza that precedes the 'Valse des Fleurs' in Tchaikovsky's *Casse Noisette* suite is a superb example of how to give an impression of splendour without using conventional resources such as brass fanfares.

Having started this orchestra survey with a page showing the standard 'classical' orchestra of the late eighteenth and early nineteenth centuries, it is only right to finish with one showing the disposition of the many additional instruments we have encountered on the way. Not all will be required for every work on a programme; many a time an 'extra' such as the bass clarinettist will sneak quietly onto the platform for one work and then make his way home, to the envy of his colleagues.

In recent times the symphony orchestra is showing signs of disintegration; composers have grown tired of accepting a combination that has preserved the same grouping for the best part of a hundred years. Consequently, a number of works have been written which experiment with new formations, breaking away from the conventional seating plan and dividing the players into mixed groups that could well have a violin, cello, trumpet, flute and xylophone sitting in one area, a horn, trombone, clarinet, viola, harp and double bass in another. The stereophonic effects achieved by placing groups in different parts of the hall have also become something of a vogue. Such novelties may be new in effect but are immensely old in precedent, since oddly mixed assortments of instruments date back to the Middle Ages, while the antiphonal opposition of instrumental sounds was much exploited by Venetian composers such as Gabrieli. To preside over the dissolution of the orchestra at this stage would be depressing; having at least assembled our resources, let us now see how best they may be combined.

6

Blending the Colours

The art of orchestration might be compared to the painter's use of colours; these may be bright or sombre, clear or indistinct, harsh or bland. Just as a painter has the ability to see analytically colours that the layman takes for granted, so must the composer be able to build up a tonal 'picture' in his mind. He will know how to bring a theme to the foreground or to remove a harmony to the background; he will have a sense of tonal perspective, knowing how to make sounds seem distant or close. He must appreciate the relative densities of sound, keeping something in reserve for climaxes and avoiding the stodginess that can come with an excess of 'doubling'. He must also be keenly aware of the relativity of pitch, of the fact that the words 'high' and 'low' are meaningless in orchestral terms unless applied specifically. ('Middle' C on the piano is a very 'high' note for a double bass, a very 'low' note for a flute.) He will not write music in the abstract and then transfer it to the orchestra; the proper sound is inherent in the original thought, though inevitably a certain amount of filling-in is unavoidable.

Let us begin with the simplest idea, a single chord; G major will do, the one that gets an audience on to its feet before the National Anthem. By the judicious and imaginative blending of orchestral sounds we can make even so familiar a musical object as this reveal an astonishing range. Since the day begins in darkness let us do the same. Where are the dark sounds? Double basses, cellos, violas, bassoons, low clarinets, bass clarinet, trombones, tuba, low horns; like so many ingredients on a chef's table they are all there to be mixed and blended according to taste. (To make things easier I shall write everything at actual pitch, untransposed.) Let's start at the bottom with double basses.

'div. a 3' is shorthand for 'divisi a tre', divided into three. Assuming we have a full symphony orchestra with, for reasons of mathematical convenience, twelve players in the bass section, this would mean four players on each of the three notes in the chord. The sound would be extremely muddy and

74

unpleasant and I doubt if any composer in his right mind would use it. Berlioz admittedly divides his double basses into four in the *Symphonie Fantastique* but to very special purpose; either he uses them pizzicato, as a way of deepening and amplifying the sound of drums, or, in the finale, he gives them a sort of subterranean grumble that must have excited feelings of sheer terror in his audience. Lesson One, then, is to avoid close formations of harmony in extreme bass registers. Let us try spacing the chord out and bringing in some cellos, divided and muted (*con sordini*). Mutes make the sound more veiled and mysterious.

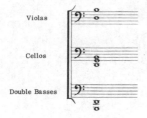

By cutting down the number of double basses we have made the sound less turgid; to have the top basses and lower cellos playing the same note will help to fuse the different tone colours. The spacing we now have will be beautiful and slightly nebulous; suppose that we want to add a darker tinge like a thin streak of black cloud in a dawn sky. Add bassoons to the cellos; even if you mark them *ppp*, they will not be able to play anything like as quietly as the strings; they will stand out, giving a slightly sinister tone – the sort of effect Sibelius often exploited. A bass clarinet would be gentler, more 'breathy' in tone, grey cloud rather than black. To lift the chord a little out of the depths, adding lightness, bring in violas, also muted and *divisi*

By now the tonic note G needs a little reinforcement, so we might add a couple of 'stopped' horns (muted by pushing the hand well into the bell of the instrument). It is one of the quietest sounds in the orchestra, with a distant magic to it. Give them these notes:

They will simply reinforce the upper partials of the low G in the double basses without obtruding in any way. Whatever happens, don't let your violins play the G below middle C. It will be an open string and will stick out like the proverbial sore thumb since the tone cannot be sweetened with vibrato.

Bringing in more light as dawn progresses, we might add a couple of flutes fairly low down; in this register they will be able to play more quietly than oboes could and their tone will match rather well with the stopped horns.

If we want to increase the daylight still more, we could add more woodwind at this point, but remember that the sound is going to be top-heavy unless we build its foundations up. We should add the remaining double basses, perhaps putting them all onto the bottom G only; we should un-stop those horns and bring in two more players to make a complete G major chord; we should interleave the oboes and clarinets so that the colours in our tonal spectrum are not too clearly separated. Our chord will now be looking like this:

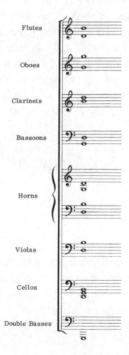

If we want to bring the sun out, the violins could do a lovely crescendo, helped by an introductory harp glissando and a shimmer of light from a suspended cymbal with soft timpani sticks playing a roll on its rim. Move the flutes up to the G to give brightness, redistribute the oboes and clarinets so that the oboes strengthen the central part of the harmony while the upper G on the clarinet will blend with, but also give support to, the lower flute. Open the horn chord a bit so that the first horn now has a higher, more penetrating note; move the violas up to share the tremolando effect with violins; allow the cellos a bit of movement to match the increased activity above them.

Now I need hardly say that this is not composition but a very elementary demonstration of the use of what might be termed primary sound. Nevertheless it gives some indication of the way the aural imagination has to learn its

trade. Orchestration is a craft, and the composer must learn by experience rather than by experiment. It would be wearisome to pursue the chord of G major further; one hardly has to be told that it could be made glorious with full brass or menacing with low muted trombones, tuba, contra bassoon and a grumble on the bass drum.

One is told in the text-books that woodwind chords are always the better for being dove-tailed, so that one avoids tonal separation; but then one remembers how effectively Sibelius uses chains of thirds in his wind parts and realizes that rules are made to be broken. What cannot be forgotten is the vital matter of pitch; flutes cannot play quietly at the top of their compass nor loudly at the bottom; conversely bassoons cannot play quietly at the bottom of their compass nor loudly at the top. Every instrument has its quota of good or not-so-good sounds and these the composer must sense; he may want to use the not-so-good ones for grotesque or exaggerated purposes – they are not forbidden. It is as well to remember the players, though; they welcome everything that is interesting to do and appreciate passages that lie well under the fingers. To take another very simple example, accompanying figures such as this are a very common occurrence:

If the top line is automatically given to the second violins and the lower part to the violas it will be boring for both. It is not hard to devise a variant:

The sound will be *almost* identical – not exactly because there will be minute changes of tone-colour as first the violins and then the violas play the upper note; but how much more interesting the part has now become for the player, keeping him alert instead of causing him to sink into apathy.

The example above is an eighteenth-century cliché, but if we look at the start of Walton's First Symphony we can see how brilliantly he takes the absolutely basic idea of a bare fifth (B flat—F) and despite constant repetition converts it into something that is both thrilling to hear and challenging to play.

When it comes to dealing with the full orchestra it is possible in many cases to break down the texture into three components, top, middle and bottom, or tune, accompaniment and bass. Not surprisingly this leads to the formula 'tune' on violins and upper woodwind, 'accompaniment' on middle strings, middle wind, horns, perhaps with restrained trombones, and 'bass' on cellos, basses, bassoons, with occasionally a tuba to help out. Obviously this is a gross over-simplification, but it is a musical syndrome that composers have often felt they must avoid precisely because it is so temptingly easy. It is for this reason that we find important themes in Brahms's symphonies first appearing in the violas and cellos rather than the violins, or Schubert giving the second subject of the 'Unfinished' Symphony to the cellos with a woodwind accompaniment. No composer of quality is content merely to copy what others have done; the orchestra as a collective instrument may be essentially the same as that used by his predecessors or contemporaries, but he will constantly be searching for some new combination of tones that he can look on as truly his own. In the remainder of this book we will be looking in much closer detail at a group of symphonic works representative of various periods and styles. We may be sure that in no case did the composer look for a solution to his problems in a text-book on orchestration. The sounds were born in his mind; they were heard, transcribed and then perhaps more consciously elaborated by craftsmanship. That craftsmanship at least we can analyse even though we may not be able to begin to grasp the intensity of inner experience that a great composer undergoes as a symphony is born.

Part II

Although it is hoped that the combination of text and examples will be sufficient for full understanding, it will unquestionably be to the reader's advantage to have a miniature score to hand. The scores of works as popular as these are easily obtainable from most of the larger public libraries or may perhaps be borrowed from any music-lover enthusiastic enough to have a small private collection. Otherwise they may be purchased from any good music shop.

7

Mozart
Symphony in G Minor
No. 40 (K.550) *First movement*

1 Flute
2 Oboes
(2 Clarinets)
2 Bassoons

2 Horns
(no Trumpets)
(no Timpani)

Strings

Generally estimated to be the most profoundly emotional of all Mozart's orchestral works, this symphony has an especial interest in the context of this book since it exists in two authentic versions, the first without, the second with, clarinets. As we have seen, the clarinet came into general usage towards the end of Mozart's all too short life. The G minor symphony was written during the necessarily transitional period when clarinets were becoming available in sufficient numbers to begin to be regarded as a standard component of the orchestra rather than as an exotic extra. Mozart, who had been greatly taken with the artistry of Anton Stadler, clearly welcomed this new development, realizing at once that here was an instrument admirably fitted to blend with either bassoons or flutes according to which register was used. A comparison of the two versions shows that in approximately sixty bars he took out the oboes and put in clarinets instead, whereas the original oboe parts are left unsullied in less than fifteen bars. In all the remaining passages in the first movement incorporating the woodwind clarinets are invariably added, usually to thicken the harmony, but sometimes to double a bassoon theme an octave higher or to support a flute (or oboe) part an octave lower. The movement thus reveals an almost total conversion to clarinet tone in preference to the oboe, a conversion dictated not by considerations of volume but of blend.

Except for a last poignant turn of phrase at the end, the first sixteen bars are given to the strings only, the first and second violins playing in unison an octave apart. To support the main theme, whose inherent pathos is so subtly conveyed by falling pairs of quavers and touching silences, Mozart requires a basis of G minor harmony. Nothing could better illustrate the point already made on page 78 than his inspired solution. All that is needed in purely functional terms is some routine formula such as this:

Instead, Mozart divides his violas – in itself an unusually adventurous gamble for the period – and gives them a figure that is not only a technical challenge calculated to keep the players alert, but is also a means of conveying a continuous, if repressed, agitation that propels the music forward, denying the violins any sentimentality in which they might be tempted to indulge. As for the bass, it is sketched in so delicately with a mere touch on the first beat of each bar until, in bar 11, a sustained line begins, adding

considerable expressive power. The first entry of the woodwind (bar 14) is accompanied by chromaticisms that generate sufficient harmonic tension to provoke a loud outburst of dissonant chords scored for full wind (with horns) reinforced by drum-like repetitions of the dominant (D) from all the strings in unison. (See opposite).

There are several points worth mentioning here. Surprisingly Mozart only asks for a single flute, though I doubt if he would have turned down the offer of a second player had one been forthcoming. Even so, he resists the temptation to reinforce it with an oboe since the top C sharp and D would have been difficult, if not impossible, to play in tune. The oboe parts therefore remain as in the original score; the clarinets are added to thicken the harmony, but notice that they move in contrary motion to the oboes, supporting the rise in the flute part. Although the wind parts are not exactly interleaved in the textbook fashion, the first clarinet doubles up the first bassoon, and the second clarinet doubles the flute, perfectly illustrating the blending function Mozart had in mind for them.

The horn parts are worth noting; to the uninitiated eye the notes look distinctly wrong. Both instruments appear to begin on the same note but then move to a dissonance (E/D) which makes no sense with the surrounding harmony. The answer of course is that Mozart has prudently chosen to use horns in two keys, one in B flat, the other in G. Remembering the rule that the nominated key-note of a horn part, be it F, A, D or whatever, is always written as C, we then realize that though to the eye it appears that the two horns begin on the same note, it is actually different for each player. To the first horn, 'written' C means B flat, to the second horn, 'written' C means G; properly transposed the two parts make sense.

It is for this reason that while two wind parts may, for space-saving reasons, be written on a single stave, the two horn parts must be given a stave each.

Bar 20 sees both the end of the outburst shown above (p. 84) and the start of a reprise of the opening material. (Note the sombre touch of colour added by the bassoons' transitional phrase.) To call this ensuing section a reprise is to fall into the trap Mozart so neatly prepares, for far from being a trite repetition it is an extension that leads to dramatically new events. We are given little warning of what lies ahead, but at least we should appreciate the completely new colouring given to the initial theme by the superimposition of sustained chords first from two oboes and then, as the harmony shifts, the addition of two bassoons. Here is precisely that true art of orchestration for which we looked in vain in the Brandenburg Concertos, the sustaining of focal points of harmony in the wind while the strings continue their forward impulse. Suddenly (bar 28) the mood is transformed with the introduction of this theme.

Mozart's scoring of this is intriguing to say the least. One might be forgiven for thinking that he would wish to reinforce those accentuated crotchets by doubling them up in the wind parts. Not a bit of it; the reinforcement comes from the second violins who, forsaking their station an octave below, come to join the firsts at the same pitch. The woodwind are given strong sustained chords, one to each bar, thereby giving the music a massive quality quite different from the fragility and pathos of the opening pages. Mozart gives all the emphasis he can to the start of this new idea by giving a two-note chord to the violins and by bringing in the first horn on the initial two notes B flat—F. (Remember that they are unobtainable on the second horn since it is differently tuned.) So far, then, we have the main new theme on violins topped by clanging chords from the wind and reinforced where possible with a horn. There would be a serious danger of musical constipation if it were left at that; fully aware of the need for a continuous driving force, Mozart gives bassoons, violas, cellos *and* basses an energetic figure in quavers that gives immense vitality to the whole passage. Soon (bar 34), the whole orchestra is involved in the biggest climax so far; the driving quavers are converted into a somewhat angular scale-passage in violins (now an octave apart again), while the basic harmony is sustained by a combination of oboes, second clarinet, second bassoon, horns and the lower strings. As for the flute, the first clarinet and first bassoon, they perform a function not all that dissimilar from the sustaining pedal on a piano, holding the first note of the violins' scale throughout the bar only to yield on the final note.

The storm soon blows itself out. There is a bar's silence and then the true second subject appears, suave and elegant. The orchestration here is implicit with courtesy, a dialogue of the politest kind in which roles are duly reversed the better to convey the formality of the exchange.

Bar		Bar	
44	Strings only	52	Wind only
45	Wind answer[1]	53	Strings answer
46–50	Strings finish the phase and initiate a chromatic extension	54–5	Wind finish the phrase
		56	BUT – chromatic
		57	extension now on strings
51	Unison wind forge a link to		with oboe above

The music is interchangeable between the two columns until bar 58 when it takes a new turn, modulating to the hitherto unvisited key of A flat major, a step graciously confirmed by the flute and the two bassoons in a series of gentle syncopated A-mens. The addition of the two horns initiates a crescendo that successfully extricates us from this alien territory and brings us back triumphantly to B flat, the second subject key. A forceful chromatic scale follows:

Here Mozart uses a standard orchestral device for adding excitement. The lower strings and the two bassoons play the bottom line as written; the violins intensify the rhythmic drive by duplicating the notes in repeated quavers, thereby preventing a possible moment of stagnation on the minim D.

In bars 70–2 we find a simple descending scale in thirds, as conventional a gesture as you could find. A number of possibilities would strike any composer at such a point – violins only, two clarinets only (it goes too low for oboes), violins *and* clarinets, or violins topped by a flute an octave above. Mozart's solution is sheer enchantment, the violins close-coupled a third apart with a flute an octave above and a solo bassoon an octave below. The gap of two octaves between the flute and bassoon isolates the wind tone, giving both clarity and variety of colour to a passage that could so easily sound pedestrian. There follows one of the most exquisite moments in the whole movement; clarinet and bassoon in turn remind us of the opening theme by toying with a three-note fragment:

Second violins provide a gently burbling accompaniment, while the master-touch is revealed in an exchange between the first violins and the lower strings based on the same falling figure but here hugely extended.

---

[1] Clarinet and bassoon in unison; originally oboe and bassoon.

87

Some interesting questions about balance are raised here; clearly the dialogue between the two parts should sound equal yet the answering line in the bass is played by violas, cellos *and* double basses, the basses, needless to say, sounding an octave lower. This is roughly equivalent to an operatic ensemble in which a solo soprano is matched against two baritones and a bass in unison – scarcely an equal match.

Knowing what we do about the constitution of orchestras in Mozart's time, the doubling of the viola and cello parts would seem to be justified on numerical grounds alone. However, I think a strong case can be made for omitting the double basses at this point so that the single line of the violin part is answered by a single line from violas and cellos, indistinguishably blended. The return of the double basses to the fray in the immediately ensuing *forte* would only serve to enhance its impact. This suggestion may seem unbearably presumptuous, but we have already seen (pp. 67–8) that double bass parts were frequently 'edited' by the players on the spot for technical reasons; is it not just as probable that the players were accustomed to being told by the composer-conductor to drop out for a few bars for valid musical reasons? The same problem occurs to an even greater degree when the passage reappears a few bars later with roles reversed, the B flat—A given to the lower strings, the E flat—D given to the violins. Since the violas cannot play the low B flat—A, Mozart is compelled to put them an octave above the cellos. Does it really make musical sense to have a further octave split with the double basses growling away below the bass stave?

If the basses are to play here, it would seem preferable that they should at least duplicate the actual pitch of the cellos; the music is too delicate in substance to tolerate the somewhat over-weighted bottom line shown above. If such proposals sound akin to blasphemy I would say in my defence that composers of the day used every shorthand device available to cut down on the sheer manual labour involved in writing a score. To write cello and bass parts on separate staves was extremely rare, and although one does occasionally find the instruction 'senza basso' or its equivalent, I cannot believe that there were not occasions when the composer used his discretion to make adjustments of this kind in rehearsal. It is said that Mozart wrote his last three symphonies in the space of six weeks, a feat incredible enough in itself without expecting him to be too fussy about details of the sort raised here.

The closing bars of the exposition (85–100) are scored for full orchestra, one surprising feature being the absence of timpani. Mozart aims for the biggest sound practicable by writing brilliant scale passages that are played in unison by all the wind and strings together. The conventional tonic and dominant chords are then hammered home to establish the landmark of the double-bar with its obligatory injunction to turn back to the first page and repeat. The convention having been duly observed, two abrupt chords project us almost brutally into the development.

This is remarkable in every way; in the first place it begins in a key so alien that the ear can hardly accept it. F sharp minor after G minor gives the impression that the entire orchestra has suddenly gone a semitone flat. The drift into this foreign key is made more acceptable by a sustained descent in the woodwind. Flute and oboe (a third apart) are matched exactly by two bassoons a couple of octaves beneath them. It is worth pointing out that this is one of the very rare occasions when Mozart preserved his original scoring in a woodwind passage, resisting the temptation to incorporate clarinets. To have put them into the intervening gap would have thickened the phrase unnecessarily, while to have given the upper chain of thirds to two oboes to match the two bassoons below would have been courting disaster since the top part would lie perilously high. As it is, the blend of a single flute and oboe combines clarity and poignancy most effectively.

Although, apart from the curious change of tonality already mentioned, the opening material now seems to be scored much as it was before, we should not disregard the sombre shadow cast by sustained bassoon chords whose subtly changing intervals emphasize the feeling of a gradual descent into a more threatening world. It is reached at bar 114, the dramatic core of the movement in which Mozart seems to fling his material into the melting-pot. For more than thirty bars he sustains a remarkable sense of conflict between three elements. They are the first theme of the movement (now shorn of pathos), a choppy and aggressive counterpoint in staccato quavers and, thirdly, syncopated dissonances in the woodwind. The first and second elements are tossed turn and turn about between the violins and the lower strings, reinforced throughout by the bassoons. The upper wind parts, flute, oboes and clarinets, consist essentially of simple two-part writing, doubled up to achieve maximum volume.

From bar 126 onward the wind parts become more continuously sustained, and it is at this climax that one feels the absence of trumpets and timpani most. This is evident from the horn parts, which consist of any notes that Mozart worked out they could usefully provide from the rather limited choice available.

The development section of this movement can be divided more or less into two halves, the first turbulent, the second anguished. As is so often the case, we are struck by the inherently operatic character of the music, the furious recriminations of the male being so touchingly answered by the female, at first timorously and then with her pleading intensified by grief. For eight bars Mozart keeps referring to the initial subject of the movement in the first violins alone – a most unusual piece of scoring in itself. The response to each phrase comes from the woodwind, flute and first clarinet (a third apart) exactly matching the pattern of the violins, while the second clarinet and first bassoon sustain a dark thread of tone that can scarcely be described as harmony, its function being comparable to a restraining hand against the piteous sighs emanating from above. The nakedness of the scoring in this section (bars 139–46) is extraordinarily touching, but the emotional intensity is soon increased by a quite new treatment of the opening material, now richly harmonized in the strings with plangent echoes in the wind.

Interestingly enough, Mozart does specify cellos alone on the bottom line here since not only does the part lie a little too high for the average bass-player of his day, but also the sense of anguish is enhanced by the strings being close-packed in harmony. (We *clasp* our hands in grief.) At bar 153 the music grows clamorous in protest and here Mozart uses his horns to splendid effect, reiterating the dominant of G minor (D) like some great tolling bell. Although there is basically only one harmony to each bar, he manages to convey a positive wildness of emotion by moving the wind parts in contrary motion while at the same time setting up a conflict between the three upper strings and the cellos – now rejoined by the double basses to give them extra strength. It is the ultimate peak of tension in the movement, emotionally and harmonically. The release comes unforgettably with a chromatic descent scored for woodwind alone leading to the recapitulation. Once again a comparison of the two versions shows Mozart preferring clarinets to oboes.

A composer of Mozart's calibre would feel he was failing to measure up to his own high standards of craftsmanship were he to allow the recapitulation to pursue its course with no new interest for the listener. The difference does not need to be spectacular; indeed that would be improper, for it would destroy the feeling of regaining familiar ground that is part of the pleasure to be derived from the reprise. A simple bassoon counter-melody spread over some five bars is enough to give a completely new slant to the opening material, the sustained line acting as a true foil to the plaintive yet breathless theme which has grown so familiar during the course of the movement.

From bar 187 onwards the listener needs to be aware of innumerable subtle changes. The theme quoted on p. 86 must for structural reasons now appear in E flat major instead of B flat; this necessitates a diversion, towards which the woodwind lend a guiding hand. (Notice a particularly effective C flat in the flute part of bar 188.) This secondary but vigorous theme is accorded a treatment that differs in a number of ways. Where originally the woodwind had one clanging chord to each bar we now find the flute encouraging his brother wind-players to introduce two chords to the bar, and chromatic ones at that. The aggressive theme, once the sole prerogative of the violins, is transferred dramatically to the lower strings and bassoons while the wind sustain a complex web of harmony against an energetic scale-based figure in the violins. Soon an intense argument develops between the first violins and the lower strings. Notice the dramatic leaps in the violin part, a sure sign of deep agitation.

Couple this with powerful wind chords on the subsidiary beats of each bar, potent blasts from both horns and a continuation of the busy quaver figuration in the second violins and you have Mozartian orchestration at its most dramatic. One senses that everyone is at full stretch for more than thirty bars, the silent bar which ends the section genuinely signalling exhaustion, emotional and physical.

The second subject, now in G minor, is scored with an exchange of courtesies comparable to that shown diagrammatically on p. 87, the change from major to minor with all that that implies bringing sufficient variation. Indeed from this point to the end of the movement the similarities of orchestration are sufficiently numerous to lull the inattentive listener into a feeling that all is proceeding according to expectation. It is precisely at such moments one should be on one's guard, for within the last eighteen bars Mozart has several major surprises in store. The first is an extraordinary chromatic ascent in which the wind lead and the strings follow, except for the violas and second horn, who between them hammer away relentlessly at the tonic-note G.

This, within the limitations of the idiom of 1784, is as powerful as anything in Beethoven. After its violence, a tranquil cadence in the wood-wind seems to be leading us to a quiet resolution, a surmise that is encouraged by the next unexpected development – a completely new treatment of the opening theme. Gone is the restless quaver accompaniment from the violas; instead we find a serenely beautiful counterpoint based on a falling scale together with a bass-line of grave simplicity. It is a moment to which even the stoniest heart must surely respond as the strings are given an

opportunity to demonstrate a sustained sweetness of tone so far denied them.

Tempting though a quiet ending may have been at such a moment, it was not to be, and Mozart, eschewing sentimentality, thumps home the tonality of G minor in the closing seven bars. Despite his amazing facility there has not been a bar that lacks distinction nor a wasted note. It is all too easy for us to take such perfection for granted; he did not, and his willingness to revise the score to include clarinets (a very unusual step for him to take) gives us an incontestable reminder that even after having composed a masterpiece he would still seek to improve it if he could. He did not change the musical content in any way; he changed the orchestration, and that only because he felt that an orchestra with clarinets was better than one without. In his determination to be subtle he rejected those orchestral rowdies, the trumpets and the kettledrums; they were unquestionably available but he preferred not to use them in a work so personal in its expression. One could choose a thousand examples to demonstrate Mozart's imaginative mastery of the orchestra; if I have chosen this particular movement, it has been partly because sundry debased versions have gained currency in recent years. To add jangling guitars and a plodding rhythm section to music of such exquisite perfection is an act of musical vandalism of which our society should feel profoundly ashamed.

8

Beethoven
Symphony No.2 in D, op. 36. *The scherzo*

2 Flutes, 2 Oboes, 2 Clarinets, 2 Bassoons
2 Horns, 2 Trumpets
2 Timpani
Strings

This combination of instruments is what might be termed the standard classical orchestra; such additions as were made – an extra pair of horns, a trio of trombones, a piccolo or percussion instruments of some kind – were initially brought in for special effects and were often reserved for one movement only. (Berlioz, not notable for economic foresight, asks for two harps in the second movement *only* for his Fantastic Symphony, for two tubas in the third movement only, for bells only in the finale.) But even Beethoven, whose orchestral requirements were normally entirely reasonable, expected (in the Fifth Symphony) that a piccolo-player, three trombonists and one contra-bassoonist should sit tacitly through the first three movements before making their presence felt. In the Sixth Symphony the trumpets and trombones are employed only in the Storm and the Finale, while in the Ninth Symphony it is not only the soloists and chorus who have to wait until the last movement to make their contribution but also the percussion players (three of them), the piccolo and the contra-bassoon. Lest it seem that I am quoting too many exceptions to make a rule worth proving, it should be emphasized that the 'standard' orchestra specified at the head of this chapter stood him in perfectly good stead for Symphonies 1, 2, 4, 7 and 8.

It may seem perverse to pick on the scherzo of one of the less frequently performed of his symphonies as a significant example. My reason for doing so is that whereas in the Mozart movement we have just explored the orchestral texture was beautifully interwoven, here we find an emphasis on separation. It is a scherzo whose sound is quite unusually spare, so much so that we feel almost as though a schoolmaster, confronted with a recalcitrant class, was to point a finger demandingly at first one then another of his pupils, making each in turn stand up to blurt out a timid answer to his searching questions. In other words Beethoven is asking for very quick responses from his players. At the brisk tempo implied by a pulse of one beat to the bar, rests must be counted positively, the players constantly alert for the next entry. Hesitation for even a fraction of a second can bring disaster not just to the culprit but to all around him. Assuming that each bar lasts something like two-thirds of a second ($\downarrow$. = 100), one can see the problem Beethoven has devised by looking at it in diagrammatic form.

Bar	1(*f*) full orchestra	2(*p*) 1st violins only	3(*f*) full orchestra	4(*p*) 1st violins only	5(*p*) horns only	6(*p*) 1st and 2nd violins
	7(*p*) oboes and horns	8(*ff*) full orchestra (less horns)	9(*f*) full orchestra (with horns)	10(*p*) 1st violins only	11(*f*) full orchestra	12(*p*) 1st violins only
	13(*p*) oboes 2nd violins and violas	14(*p*) 1st and 2nd violins	15(*p*) flutes oboes bassoons horns	16(*ff*) full orchestra		

The kaleidoscopic effect of these continually changing sonorities is enhanced by the fact that each three-crotchet phrase within the bar is complete in itself; there is no overspill from one bar into the next to smooth over the joins – indeed there are no joins, just abrupt statements, sometimes aggressive, sometimes tentative. The doh-re-mi pattern from which it all springs could scarcely be simpler but the treatment is unusual and adventurous.

As a foil to these rapid changes we now find eight bars for strings only, interrupted at the last moment by the wind, who pick up a syncopated accent and a subsequent flight of quavers from them, thus super-imposing four bars of woodwind colour as a different type of contrast. It is worth mentioning that the bassoon drops out when it comes to the rapid quaver passage; Beethoven no doubt felt that it really would be asking for trouble to expect such agility from a somewhat clumsy instrument in the hands of a possibly inexpert player. In the Fourth Symphony, written some four years later, he was to have no such inhibitions, giving the bassoonist a notoriously difficult solo in the finale which to this day is awaited eagerly by sadistic connoisseurs in much the same spirit as that of people who watch motor-racing primarily for the accidents.

Ten bars of feverish but suppressed activity from the strings bring us back to a reprise of the opening material – or so it seems for a further twelve bars during which everything goes according to plan. Suddenly and characteristically expectation is denied; first and second violins have a delightfully contradictory dialogue full of subtle changes of inflection.

The effect of this tends to be diminished to a certain extent by the modern lay-out of the orchestra in which both first and second violins sit to the conductor's left. In Beethoven's day the violins would have sat as in a string quartet, first violins to the left, seconds on the right. The passage shown above would therefore not only be stereophonic in effect but also rather more hazardous, thereby enhancing what is clearly a Beethoven joke of a kind rather more subtle than the violent juxtapositions in the opening section of the movements.

The ensuing passage is sheer delight, a pawky little tune for oboe and bassoon an octave apart accompanied with extreme delicacy by the strings until what I can only describe as a 'chromatic growl' brings a touch of mock menace from the lower strings, backed up by bassoons. The crescendo from *pp* to *f* needs to be accomplished in two bars, a transition made considerably easier by the addition of two horns sustaining an octave D but growing in intensity as they do so. For a moment the music seems to be stuck in a groove, the two bars being twice repeated. The crisis is resolved when the full orchestra comes to the rescue, rounding things off with a determined cadence.

There follows the so-called Trio in which Beethoven again seems to be more interested in contrast than blend. The initial eight bars are a beautiful demonstration of how to write for oboes and bassoons, incorporating horns when the point needs to be underlined. Since the phrase is repeated, there is in all a sixteen-bar respite from string tone. What an effect it makes, then, when all the strings in raucous unison cut into this pastoral idyll, savaging the chord of F sharp major until, feeling that their interruption has indeed been rude and unruly, their clamour dies to a whisper, finally freezing to stillness on a single held note. Unfortunately it is the wrong note as far as the rest of the orchestra is concerned; the full wind, brass and timpani blare out a great unison A to get the music back on course. It is a typical Beethoven jest, a loud guffaw at the way in which he has led us astray. Instantly, to show it was all in good fun, he re-introduces the first theme of the Trio, this time accompanied by a tiptoe scale on the bassoon. The subsequent transference of this passage to the strings with the running bass played pizzicato is one of the most elegant examples of orchestration in the whole symphony. Although pizzicato is often found in the music of Haydn and Mozart, I cannot recall a more telling instance of its use. Part of the magic is undoubtedly caused by the transference to strings in the middle register of a tune we have consistently heard played by wind in a high register; but the simple change from wind to strings is not enough to explain the special quality of this passage. By a happy chance the first horn can play the theme at the same pitch as the violins. The blend is a subtle one for, since pitch is relative to an instrument's compass, we find the intriguing mixture of a 'high' horn part corresponding to a 'low' violin part. The oboes soon remind us that it was their tune all the time and a gentle argument seems about to become more heated before flutes and clarinets add their soothing voices and bring the Trio to an uncontentious end.

The impact of the first bar of the 'da capo'[1] repeat is all the greater for coming after this gentle cadence, but it is the return to abrupt one-bar phrases after the longer melodic lines of the Trio that intensifies the contrast. It could be said that the essence of this movement lies in the juxtaposition of sections made up of one-bar units with other sections comprising four or eight bars. It is an unusual structure, a structure whose salient points are made absolutely clear by its special type of orchestral writing.

[1] Literally 'from the head', the tradition being to repeat the scherzo from the beginning and finish where the Trio began.

9

Schubert
Symphony in B Minor (The 'Unfinished')
First movement

2 Flutes, 2 Oboes, 2 Clarinets, 2 Bassoons
2 Horns, 2 Trumpets
3 Trombones (2 tenor, 1 bass)
2 Timpani

Strings

It has been said that there is no substitute for experience when it comes to learning a trade, to which I would reply that there is no substitute for genius if by circumstance experience is denied. So far as is known, Schubert never heard any of his symphonies except possibly in amateur and ill-balanced performances. His sole orchestral experience came in the theatre pit, either as a composer of ill-fated operas or as the provider of incidental music for third-rate plays. While this may have taught him something about the basics of orchestration it can have done nothing to refine his ear by practical experiment. He learned, as most composers learn, by listening; but to listen is not enough. One must not copy but invent. Stravinsky tells how once, when filling in a form at a frontier, he described himself as an 'inventor', a provocative but truthful description since it is the composer's business to invent sound. All the same it could be argued that much of the language of music consists of acceptable clichés, whether the formula accompanying figures of the eighteenth century, the scales and arpeggios that crop up so frequently in nineteenth-century piano music, the synthetic tension of tremolando diminished sevenths accompanying the misdeeds of operatic villains or the more recent cliché that demands dissonance in every chord. To every age its *lingua franca*; if we are to communicate, we need some common ground. Accept that music is a form of communication, and we must also accept that there must be familiar elements that provide a link between composer and listener. The truly great composer finds how to shed new light on the familiar; there could be no better example of this than Schubert's 'Unfinished', not a bar of which is derivative, causing an inner voice to murmur to us 'How like Beethoven . . .' or 'A touch of Mozart there!' Yet at no point does the music strike us as consciously daring in the way that the compositions of Berlioz, Wagner or Liszt do. The symphony *communicates* with such a lack of self-consciousness that it reaches straight to the heart, hence its enormous popularity. Schubert's use of the orchestra is perfection, a perfection that could be taught in no school but which stemmed from an imaginative ear that knew precisely how to achieve every effect. Experience had nothing to do with it; the work was not performed until December 17, 1865, thirty-seven years after his death.

The opening phrase, that almost inaudible sombre unison on cellos and basses, is sheer magic. Before I get carried further into hyperbole let me pinpoint a dilemma posed by the fifth bar. The cellos descend to a low D and C sharp, notes which the double basses in Schubert's day could not play at the lower octave. Schubert is compelled therefore to change the contour of the bass line, momentarily shifting into an exact unison with the cellos instead of lying an octave beneath.

Most of the double basses in the modern symphony orchestra can now take the fifth bar an octave lower, since the compass has been extended to low C instead of the E which was the bottom note available to Schubert.[1] If they do so, they preserve the consistency of the octave line beneath the cellos; on the other hand, the original line as written by Schubert has an added touch of poignancy with the rising fifth to D followed by the falling fifth to the low F sharp. Which option to choose is an artistic decision not to be taken without thought.

The gently murmuring accompanying figure which now begins in the violins is certainly a cliché, but so handled as to be continually intriguing to the ear. Written as three crotchet beats

it is shaped to give the impression of two *dotted* crotchet beats, 6/8 instead of 3/4.

The illusion is subtly supported by pizzicato cellos and basses, sounding almost like pitched timpani. The conductor needs to preserve the delicate

---

[1] In the mid-nineteenth century various experimental monster double basses were made, some so vast that they had to be played with pedal-operated levers. Like the dinosaur, they failed to survive.

ambivalence of the rhythm so that the music maintains its air of mystery, a mystery further heightened by the exact fusion of oboe and clarinet in the song-like melody which soon appears. Either a solo oboe or a solo clarinet would be clearly identifiable, as for that matter would the pair of them playing an octave apart. As it is, the soft 'woody' tone of the clarinet casts a slight shadow over the more pungent, reedy tone of the oboe so that our ears are teased by a sound that is neither one nor the other.

Before we leave the matter of the accompanying figure that continues virtually unbroken from bars 9 to 35, it is worth pointing out that however different they may be in both sound and effect, this symphony and the Mozart G minor share a common formula in the accompaniment. Mozart divides his violas, giving them swiftly repeated notes in pairs to create a nervous, even slightly agitated accompaniment. Schubert divides his violins, giving them swiftly repeated notes in pairs to create a rather more mysterious but still potentially agitated effect. The essential difference is that Mozart's accompaniment is entirely harmonic in conception while Schubert's is full of implications of melody, implications that are only fully revealed by the woodwind. (How many casual listeners appreciate that the A sharp—B—C sharp quavers that form so conspicuous a part of the woodwind melody have been subtly suggested by the murmuring strings in the preceding bars?)

No sooner has the first lyrical phrase on the woodwind ended than the mood is disturbed by a momentary shock chord from horns and bassoons, a single *sforzando* from the bass trombone adding sharpness to the impact. It should be said that Schubert is here treating the trombone as a surrogate third horn and the sound should be balanced accordingly. Although the interruption is brief, it makes its point, for while it seems that the woodwind theme resumes its leisurely course there are indications that things are not to be the same. A solo horn adds some pressure to the harmony (bars 23–5); in response to its summons the remaining woodwind add considerable density to the texture, clarinets and bassoons doubling up in thirds an octave apart reinforced by the second oboe. The second flute, first oboe and the two horns try to exercise some restraint over the gathering impetus of the phrase by sustaining a unison D, but they too must yield to the growing pressure beneath, and the music explodes into two climactic chords whose impact is greatly increased by the addition of trumpets, all three trombones and timpani. It is a classic demonstration of how to hold one's strongest forces in reserve. Even so, Schubert senses that the moment is too soon for a more full-blooded climax; horns and clarinets (an octave apart) calm things down with a sighing phrase that rocks gently from G to the F sharp a semitone below only to find the forces regathering their strength and building towards the true climax (bars 36–8).

The scoring here is full of interest. The dominating rhythm is powerful, while still preserving the ambiguity that has been so notable a feature.

♩ ⁊♪♩ |⁊♪♩ ♫|♩ ⁊ ⁊ |

doesn't sound like 3/4 because the ear will tend to interpret it as

♩ ⁊♪|♩ ⁊♪|♩ ♫|♩ ⁊

The conductor may interpret this in two ways, either as an implied break into 2/4, with the effect of urgency which that implies, or as a massive 3/2 spread over the two bars, in which case the effect is one of expansion. Now Schubert could well have duplicated this rhythm in all parts; instead, he gives us a sustained harmony held over two bars in the woodwind and horns, serving something akin to the function of the sustaining pedal on the piano. The rhythm is hammered out by trumpets, timpani and full strings. It is the trombone part that reveals his care for detail. The obvious, unthinking reaction of the mediocre composer would be to give the trombones the same dramatic rhythm as the trumpets and strings. Schubert preferred to limit them to this:

|♩ ⁊ ♩ |⁊ ♩. ♪|♩ ⁊ ⁊

Why? Not I believe just to hammer out the cross-accentuation even more relentlessly but because he took into account the problem of ensemble that would arise were they to duplicate exactly the rhythm so forcibly enunciated by trumpets, timpani and strings. Different instruments take different times to 'speak' and the chances were that had the trombones been given the upbeat quavers as well, they might easily have lagged fractionally behind the trumpets, making the passage sound ragged rather than forceful.

Now genius though he was, Schubert's natural inclination to follow his lyrical muse could sometimes create problems that a more cerebrally inclined composer would avoid. The climax which we have just reached is a totally convincing gesture in terms of musical rhetoric yet it suffers from a severe drawback if we consider it as part of a symphonic structure. Magnificent though it may be, it is in the wrong key for the situation. With the imminent arrival of the second subject (almost certain to be in the relative major (D), a tonality whose relationship is easily comprehended since it shares the same key signature of two sharps), the last thing we need is so undeniable an assertion of the tonic key, B minor. An orthodox composer would have arranged things more efficiently so that this splendid climax would have established the dominant of the new key, thereby opening the door to the second subject. In terms of tonality, and tonality was fundamental to the whole concept of symphonic form, Schubert's journey has brought him nowhere; he has merely re-affirmed the key he started from. His solution to the dilemma is inspired. Out of the massive B minor chord emerges a single note, D – the third note of the B minor scale. It is scored for bassoons and horns in unison, though I am reasonably certain that if he had had four horns available, he would have used them in preference to the mixture of wind and brass tone. He holds the note for nine whole beats to keep us in suspense; where is he going? Orthodoxy demands that he should make for D major, in fact a perfectly practical move.

It works, but the emotional release of the new key is diminished by the unsubtle way in which it is proclaimed. Instead, with a tonal shift of a kind he made peculiarly his own, he treats the sustained D as the dominant of G major, into which quite unexpected key he effortlessly glides. Where convention dictates a modulation *up* a minor third to the relative major, he modulates *down* a major third to its sub-dominant. Having achieved his unexpected goal, he sets up a gently syncopated accompaniment.

Consider the possibilities that even this simple formula offers. The matching thirds, spaced an octave apart, could perfectly well be played by any of the following combinations:

a violins	*b* flutes	*c* oboes	*d* clarinets	*e* clarinets
violas	clarinets	bassoons	horns	cellos

Bearing in mind that he proposes to give the tune beneath this accompaniment to the cellos, Schubert almost certainly rejected *a* as too alike in colouring. The theme might merge into its background. *b* is attractive, but the clarinets with their rather sombre lower register might be in danger of obscuring the cellos, which would be in close proximity. *c* can be dismissed as too sharply pungent for so discreet an accompaniment even though the blend of reed instruments would be perfectly tolerable in itself. *d* has distinct possibilities, always assuming that the required notes could be played by the horns. Since the passage modulates, this would almost certainly cause problems. *e* would produce a nice texture, but must clearly be discounted if the cellos are intended to play the tune. In proposing these alternatives I am not suggesting that Schubert went through the laborious process of trial and error implied; his solution, clarinets in the upper octave, violas in the lower, is the perfect one, though it was probably devised instinctively. The clarinets can give just the right amount of weight to the upper line while the violas make a pleasing but unobtrusive intermediary between the wind tone of the clarinets and the string tone of the cellos. The

102

pizzicato double basses provide all that is needed to register the first beats, both rhythmically and harmonically.

Once the tune is taken over by the violins (firsts and seconds in unison an octave apart), Schubert adds a little more definition to the accompaniment by substituting bassoons for violas; furthermore – and this is a true master-stroke of orchestration – he brings in the two horns with extreme delicacy in such a way that their deftly-placed syncopations cross the bar line, linking each harmony to the next. The final touch of genius is the cello part, now deprived of the tune, but nodding quiet approval of the violins by echoing the essential aspects of the melody. Just as the tune seems about to flower, it fades into silence; we wait, expectant.

Without warning Schubert launches a musical thunderbolt. The entire orchestra save only the timpani blares out a huge chord of C minor, a fearsome contradiction of what has gone before. The absence of the timpani can easily be explained. Schubert has only the two, tuned to B and F sharp, neither note being compatible with this alien harmony. Later in the move-ment a directly comparable passage occurs, this time in a key in which the timpani can be used. Needless to say he takes advantage of this and includes them. Again an interpretative question is raised: should we provide the timpani rolls which appear to be lacking at this first thunderclap, since the required notes present no problem to the modern timpanist, or do we rather argue that the omission of the timpani on the first occasion keeps something in reserve to make an even greater impact the second time? There is merit in both views; personally I am rather in favour of supplying the 'missing' timpani, if only because Schubert indisputably meant the chord to create a profound shock. The addition of timpani not shown in the score might succeed in recreating something of the original impact of that shock in the minds of those listeners who imagine that they know the symphony so well that nothing can surprise them any more.

Schubert, nature-poet that he was, may well have been inspired by thunder when he decided to interrupt the sweet flow of his second subject so violently; the same could be said of the second thunder-clap which follows. However, the work is a symphony, not a tone-poem, and this dramatic and unpredictable element is soon made eminently symphonic by an extension that has no relationship to nature. Trumpets and timpani may be omitted for reasons of practical limitation but Schubert does his utmost to compensate for their absence by marking every beat with a heavy accent. (At the later occurrence of the comparable passage both trumpets and timpani are able to participate.)

The music builds to the loudest climax yet (bar 71) – notice how he manages to fit in the trumpets on the final note – before dissolving into two bars of woodwind harmony. The syncopations, restless at first, settle down into quietly sustained chords against which the strings begin an elegantly poised dialogue.

103

As though symbolizing that such old-fashioned courtesies have no place in a modern world, Schubert converts this polite exchange into a fierce argument. The full brass become embroiled, sometimes on the beat, sometimes off, while the sense of struggle is brilliantly conveyed not just by the

104

altercation between lower and upper strings but by the syncopated rhythms which are tossed from the shrill voices of flutes and oboes to the blare of horns and trombones.

Notice that of all the wind parts only the bassoons share material with the strings. Orchestras of the day tended to be bottom-light, and while the high violins could make themselves heard above the storm, cellos and violas would need all the help they could get to cut through the powerful chords from the full brass.

Dramatic though this passage may be, it is comparatively short-lived. Schubert, not a composer noted for brevity, here manages to say in sixteen bars what Beethoven might have said in sixty. That all is forgiven is made clear by the immediately ensuing passage, one of the most meltingly beautiful that even Schubert ever penned. The second subject returns, but this time it is treated contrapuntally, one part rising above the other in ecstatic descent. The bare bones can be revealed in three lines.

The highlights of these mellifluous phrases are picked out by the wood-wind who then take over, only in turn to be enhanced in beauty by the involvement of the strings, who quickly abandon the slightest suggestion of subservience. A low sustained octave from the two horns adds a touch of shadow, the whole page conjuring up the beauty of a summer evening with a radiant purity that was to be denied to more consciously impressionistic composers such as Delius or Debussy. They gave their attention to the beauty of sound whereas here we find beauty of thought.

A dramatic unison B, gradually diminishing, arrests not only our attention but the very progress of the music. Five tentative steps, plucked in unison by the strings, lead us back to the opening bars of the work. The repeat should certainly be played, as it seems for the time being that Schubert has totally forgotten the initial theme. With regard to the structure of the movement as a whole this reminder is beautifully placed, coming as it does after an exposition of 110 bars. Almost exactly 110 bars later, the exposition having been repeated, Schubert begins the development section of the movement with not just a further reprise of the initial theme but with an extensive exploration of its potential. Cellos and basses first remind us of it in a somewhat higher register (E minor instead of B minor). In its final bars the theme descends once more into the depths, taking the cellos down to their lowest note, the open string C. Here I feel there can be no doubts about employing the extended range of the modern double basses. We need to be taken into the darkest of tonal areas since we are at the threshold of one of the most remarkably orchestrated passages Schubert ever wrote. Against the low rumble of cellos and basses, tremolando,[1] the violins and violas (supported by bassoons) begin a dialogue of such bleakness that we seem to have moved into territory more familiar to Sibelius than Schubert. The huge gap of more than two octaves between the two lines gives the music a spare, gaunt quality utterly unlike anything else in the symphony. Gradually, step by chromatic step, the music is dragged up from this veritable pit until trombones and the darker-toned wind instruments at least introduce some harmony to fill in the gulf. The tension is screwed ever tighter, violins and cellos circling in anguish round the same three notes time and time again, goaded by jabbing chords from the trombones and wind. The crisis is resolved by a break-through into C sharp minor (bar 146), a release which gradually allows some of the tension to dissipate. There follows a device of the utmost subtlety, a 'memory' of the second subject in which the theme itself is notable for its absence. Flutes and clarinets remind us of the syn-copated thirds that we have come to associate with the cello theme (see p. 102; their sound is unmistakable in its evocation of that glorious tune, but the tune itself is missing. It would be hard to find a more eloquent musical symbol of lost happiness. Three times a great wave of orchestral sound batters us like the voice of Lear raging at the heavens; three times the response is not silence but rather a heartbreaking reminder of a beauty no longer attainable. Here indeed orchestration proves itself to be not an applied skill but the very means by which the implied drama is made manifest.

If in such passages the spirit seems near to fainting, there is no mistaking the message of the great orchestral unison which now materializes. Could one believe when one first heard that mysteriously veiled introductory theme that it could be capable of showing such immense power? In describing the phrase as a 'great orchestral unison' I have told less than the truth, although the impression given is indeed that of unanimity. However, to give the phrase even greater strength, trumpets and two of the trombones cling rigidly to the key-note, like an inflexible girder that supports the entire superstructure.

Now the general impression we have gained of the symphony so far is one of restrained melancholy shot through with moments of radiant beauty. Only occasionally, and that for relatively brief snatches at a time, has the music revealed a toughness of fibre. Here, at almost the exact centre point of the movement (bar 175 out of a total of 368), we find a central core of extraordinary turbulence. The prime factor in establishing this new mood is an energetic new figure in the violins and violas.

[1] The addition of a bass drum *pp* would be marvellously effective here.

To use Captain Ahab's marvellously descriptive word, it 'spiralizes', while basses, cellos and trombones thunder out the first four notes of the introductory theme, now so changed in character as to be barely recognizable. They are answered by the full choir of woodwind reinforced by trumpets and horns. How Schubert must have longed for valved brass instruments at such a moment so that there could have been an evenly matched dialogue between the trombones (who can play the theme) and the trumpets and horns who cannot. As a compensation for such inadequacies he is compelled to introduce a new rhythm

which effectively adds considerable fuel to the fire even when restricted to one note. Meanwhile upper and lower strings are engaged in a titanic struggle, the trombones tilting the balance in the cellos' favour despite an alliance between flutes, clarinets and violins. It is a climax that matches Beethoven in power without sounding in the least *like* Beethoven. Indeed there is one passage that anticipates Berlioz when all the strings in unison play this figure.

In terms of sheer orchestral technique it is well on the way towards this passage in the 'March to the Scaffold' in the *Symphonie Fantastique*:

Berlioz-like too are the sudden extreme changes of dynamic from *ff* to *pp* although they are less openly neurotic in effect.

This central climax lasts for nearly forty bars during which Schubert handles the resources of the full orchestra with a mastery quite astonishing in one with so little practical experience. It is one thing to marvel at Beethoven's ability to compose after he had lost his hearing, but he had heard a great deal of his music before that sense failed him totally. Schubert never 'heard' his symphonies except in his head; bearing this in mind one can only wonder at the skill with which he manages the transition from the massive weight of the full orchestra in bar 207 to the scarcely audible murmur of strings at the start of the recapitulation in bar 218. The vital passage is shown on pages 108–10, the immediately preceding bar having involved everyone except trumpets and timpani.

Notice first how the strings still preserve something of the agitation shown in the example on p. 107. The intervening rests convey a sense of exhaustion until at last, all strength drained, they are reduced to three isolated pizzicato notes, then silence.

The long-held note on the horns, ten bars and a bit without a breath, serves to 'freeze' the music in one place after the violent activity of the previous few pages. Meanwhile clarinets and bassoons move in parallel thirds, gradually calming down until they too come to a point of rest. Now the only movement comes from a forlorn flute and oboe. At last the *only* instrument to move is the flute; everyone else is either still or silent. So convincing is the impression that the music has run down completely that it is quite a relief to find it capable of movement again as the recapitulation whispers into life.

For a time things proceed as they did in the exposition, the necessary change of course being adopted without fuss. The arrival of the second subject brings the first notable change of orchestral colour. Where originally

the syncopated accompaniment was scored for clarinets and violas, with the tune in G major, we now find the accompanying chords given to flutes and clarinets. With the theme now in the 'proper' key of D, the whole lay-out is at a higher pitch. The new tone-colour provided by the flutes emphasizes this brighter aspect, even though the dynamic remains subdued.

If Schubert had a fault as a composer, it was to take the recapitulation too literally as a repeat of the exposition. Though there will inevitably be changes in tonality to enable the gravitational pull of the home-key to exert its influence, the actual course of events tends to remain unaltered, an indulgence Mozart, Haydn or Beethoven seldom allowed themselves. Only in the final coda (bars 328–end) does Schubert catch us truly unaware. Once more, as at the end of the exposition, the five pizzicato notes tiptoe their way down to the low B, once more the cellos and basses remind us of the mysterious introductory theme, that theme which has survived such storms as we had not dreamt of when the voyage began. But where originally its final note rested for three bars on a sustained F sharp, we now find solemn

109

chords superimposed, magically scored with a single flute outlining the cadence supported by what (to the eye) looks a far too sonorous combination of clarinets, bassoons, horns and trombones. Haltingly the strings begin a contrapuntal treatment of the theme that recalls the austere bleakness that created so memorable an effect at the start of the development. A murmur on the timpani sounds a warning note and a strange oscillation begins, rocking in distraught fashion between F sharp and the E sharp a semitone below. The music labours its way up a huge B minor arpeggio to what we imagine will be a final chord. Instead, Schubert recalls the opening three notes of the symphony no less than six times, twice on oboe and clarinet in unison, twice on flutes, violins and violas (supported by a powerfully swelling chord), and twice from its originators, the cellos and basses. These last two phrases are accompanied by funereal chords from clarinets, horns and trumpets. There is an end to these nostalgic sighs as three abrupt chords from the full orchestra cut the phrase off like an axe. A final sustained chord ends the symphony. Even here, in the penultimate bar, there is a problem for the interpreter to solve. The symbol for an accent (>) and the symbol for a decrescendo (⟩——⟩) are dissimilar only in length;

Schubert, habitually writing in the heat of inspiration, tended to make his accents much larger than most composers so that it is possible, where he is pressed for space, to confuse one sign with the other. Because of our justifiably romantic feelings about this work, a tradition has grown up among conductors to sustain the last chord with a diminuendo dying away to nothing. In doing so they appear to have misinterpreted the accent Schubert meticulously indicated in every part, wrongly believing it to be a diminuendo. The work is orchestrated with such complete assurance that I cannot believe that Schubert's skill would have deserted him in the very last two bars. Had he really wanted a diminuendo, would he have sustained all the wind, all the brass, all the strings *and* timpani to the bitter end? I think not. It would have been a simple matter to grade the final chord, extending it over several bars from which the heavier sounds could gradually have been eliminated until only the strings were left. That he did not do so seems to me conclusive evidence that he wanted the ending to be strong.

10

Berlioz
Symphonie Fantastique. *Last movement*

Piccolo, Flute (2 players)
2 Oboes
2 Clarinets (one in E flat, one in C)
4 Bassoons

4 Horns (two in E flat, two in C)
2 Cornets in E flat
2 Trumpets in E flat
3 Trombones
2 Tubas

4 Timpani (2 players)
Tubular Bells
Bass Drum, Cymbals

Strings

Although opinions may differ as to the musical qualities of this truly sensational movement, there can be no doubt that its orchestration is a *tour de force*. It is not surprising that Berlioz was to write a treatise on orchestration; he found the subject totally fascinating, revelling in sheer sound, yet meticulous in showing precisely how a particular effect was to be achieved. Ironically, he was no great instrumentalist himself, being a passable master of the guitar and the flute but little else. Despite this lack of practical skills he uses the orchestra with complete confidence, though it should be said that he admitted to considerable revisions of this famous score over the years. The music is unashamedly descriptive, more of a tone-poem than a symphonic finale as the title 'Dream of a Witches' Sabbath' clearly reveals. It was a subject that was bound to appeal to the composer's somewhat neurotic imagination, and from the very first bars he sets out to astonish us, exploiting the extremes of orchestral colour. The disposition of the opening chord is magical, violins and violas divided into eight separate parts that combine to form a close-packed but shimmering diminished seventh, the ubiquitous suspense-chord of the nineteenth century. The upper strings are muted, scarcely audible; far beneath them 'the Kraken wakes' with three ominous rumbles from cellos and basses in unison, the upper note of each brief ascending scale being reinforced by a dull thud from two timpani. In the third bar the violins' shimmer disintegrates into a wonderfully contrived imitation of the sound of flapping wings, followed by a fluttering chromatic descent as a flight of witches comes in to land. The music is astonishingly visual in conception, so much so that one feels that it might have been designed as a film-score rather than for the concert-hall. Bar 5 brings yet another extraordinary sound, cellos and basses divided into four parts with a circling figure that suggests the swirl of the witches' cloaks raising a cloud of dust. A series of gruff chords on the heavy brass (augmented by horns, bassoons and a low clarinet) suggests a barking dog followed by the shrill cry of a night-bird on flutes and oboes. None but Berlioz would have risked scoring the supporting harmony in the way he does – deep trombones and tuba playing this chord,

with four bassoons, two to a note, thickening the middle of the harmony with the E flat—F sharp shown in brackets. The effect is almost frighteningly sinister, its initial impact strengthened by divided strings whose quick disappearance only emphasizes the starkly sepulchral quality of the trombone-bassoon chord.

However eccentric his scoring may seem, Berlioz rarely miscalculates. Nevertheless, bar 8 offers an enigma since he calls for the flute and oboe to make a glissando descent of an octave, something which is technically impossible. He writes the passage in this way:

and it is easy enough to visualize what he had in mind – what Shakespeare might have called 'a dying fall'. Players sometimes fake it by playing a very rapid C major scale, although ideally, to correspond with the supporting harmony, it would be preferable to do this:

Articulation should be non-existent, precision being the last thing he intended.[1] The phrase evokes a distant rumble from the bass-drum, Berlioz

---

[1] There is also a technique known as a 'lip-bend' in which the player slackens his embouchure in such a way as to flatten the top C substantially, creating the illusion that a glissando is about to start. It is worth mentioning that Berlioz may have had a key-less flute in mind on which something much nearer to a glissando could have been obtained.

113

taking the trouble to specify that it should be played with two sponge-headed timpani sticks. A muted horn echoes the cry of the night-bird before a strangely angular rising phrase leads us back to the shimmering chords from the opening of the movement – not precisely repeated since the harmony is changed, but similarly orchestrated. There is in essence a reprise of the first eight bars or so (it is not exact) before a sudden change of tempo.

Enter the Beloved, disguised as a witch

There is no such stage-direction on the score, for the event is portrayed so vividly that words would be gratuitous. Throughout the previous four movements of the symphony we have been reminded at different times and in various ways of the theme or *idée fixe* that Berlioz associates with his ideal beloved, an ideal incarnate in the form of an Irish actress named Harriet Smithson with whom he had become besotted. At this stage he had never spoken to her, his plan being to invite her to a grand concert of his works which would include the first performance of this symphony. The original conception of the work contained no hint of witches, but before the finale was written Berlioz heard rumours that the fair Harriet (now back in England) had behaved with less than the scrupulous modesty expected of a goddess. Outraged that she should show signs of toppling off the pedestal upon which he had so adoringly placed her, he resolved to take revenge by turning her into a witch, a transformation skilfully achieved by creating a grotesque travesty of her theme. Once again we find a unique sound, the combination of bass drum, two timpani a fourth apart and a solo clarinet. The bass drum rumble suggests fear and the supernatural, the timpani suggests galloping hooves, while the solo clarinet with its cackling trills and distorted melody conveys an image fit for the brush of Hieronymus Bosch.

The witch's advent is greeted by a great baying sound from the full orchestra, a chaotic welter of conflicting rhythms and ingeniously inter-woven fragments. The compositional techniques here anticipate those used by Stravinsky in *The Rite of Spring* in that each part, while being relatively simple in itself, contributes to an overall texture of great complexity.

Discounting the first two bars which are simply a coarse bellowing E flat, it is worth studying the components of this page in detail (see p. 115). Flutes, oboes and the E flat clarinet maintain an obdurate, if agitated, E flat, a 'resistance' note against which dissonances can be formed. The second clarinet and the four bassoons add considerable bite to the initial four-note descent in the violins but then go their own way with strongly marked syncopations, accenting the second and fourth beats of the bar. (In fact the speed is such that the notes simply sound 'off-beat'.) The E flat horns hammer out a basic rhythm which their colleagues (in C) contradict emphatically. Cornets and trumpets set up a quite independent rhythm in triplets playing literally like men possessed. Trombones have yet another rhythm whose staccato repetitions are deliberately blurred by the tuba. As

for the strings, their disposition almost defies analysis. What we *hear* is a continuous, almost Bach-like pattern.

I suggest that this is Bach-like since Bach stands for Order; by splitting this continuous shape into a multitude of fragments as he does, Berlioz creates a powerful musical symbol of the disintegration of Order into Chaos. Nothing comparable to this had ever been penned before; its unorthodoxy is stunning.

A brief pause allows us to recover our breath before the ensuing dance. Here Berlioz makes wonderfully effective use of the shrill tones of the E flat clarinet. Three-note harmony is provided by two oboes and the second clarinet (in C). A piccolo adds an even sharper edge to the E flat clarinet's tone while the bassoons play rapid four-note arpeggios which produce a curious gobbling sound like indignant turkey-cocks. Although the section begins entirely in the woodwind, Berlioz deftly introduces support from violas and cellos; at first we hardly notice them but the sound gradually accumulates as more instruments are added. A swirling figure in the strings is given greater brilliance by the addition of flute and piccolo. Suddenly the full brass section enters with a thunderclap of a chord which momentarily checks all forward movement. All bedlam soon breaks loose with a strident chromatic scale (down an octave and back again) competing against frenzied repetitions of the minor third C—E flat. Trombones and tuba are silent for four bars, their extra resources being kept in reserve for an explosive climax. It is a climax that seems to throw the strings off balance, for in a moment we find them in an exposed unison passage, all off the beat. The massed forces of wind and brass put them back on course, though not without a strange disruption of the prevailing rhythm. There is a thrilling forward impulse to the music that sweeps us on mercilessly until there is a sudden freeze as cellos, basses and bassoons come to a stop on a high E flat. Slowly they begin a descent to the very depths, a passage where the double basses should certainly go down to the bottom C if it is available. For a moment or two there is absolute stillness and one can easily imagine the coven of witches crouched in a circle waiting for a signal from the bell-tower of the ruined church within whose grounds they have gathered to celebrate their Black Mass.

After all the aural shocks we have experienced so far in this truly Fantastic Symphony, one would imagine that Berlioz would be hard-pressed to find any further novelty. Now I do not know if bells had already been used in some operatic score by Meyerbeer, Weber or Spontini; it is certainly possible. However, to use bells in a symphony was unprecedented; indeed Berlioz shows that he is aware of the problem he has created by suggesting the use of a piano as an alternative. I trust that it is an option that has never been taken up since there is no adequate substitute for the metallic clang of tubular bells forcibly struck with a wooden mallet. Only two notes are needed, C and G, but Berlioz has the imaginative genius to space them at irregular intervals, as though the bell-ringer is unable to see the perverted rituals being enacted amongst the desecrated tombstones.

The pictorial images suggested by the music are astonishingly clear. No sooner has the third bell-note sounded than a single witch starts forward (violas), only to be checked imperiously by the Master of the Ceremonies – a brief explosive chord on trombones with two timpani and strings in support. Again the bells ring out, again two impetuous witches break ranks (oboe and violas), again and with even greater emphasis they are commanded to be still. For a third time the bells ring out, subdued and distant as though answering from across the valley. With a starkness that defies every rule of conventional scoring, the four bassoons and two tubas spell out the tradi-tional chant of the Dies Irae, a theme which every member of a Catholic audience would instantly recognize. Against its measured tread of one note to the bar the bells seem to chime almost at random. As soon as the first statement of the theme is finished, it is taken up at twice the speed by horns and trombones, harmonizing the chant in parallel thirds. Mocking the ancient majesty of the theme, woodwind and pizzicato strings produce a skipping travesty, a passage in which I am sure, had he ever come across such a thing, Berlioz would have used a xylophone to enhance the brittleness of the sound.

The tubas and bassoons now proclaim the second stanza of the Dies Irae with thudding off-beat pizzicato notes from cellos and basses suggesting the stamping of feet upon the ground. Once more the theme is repeated double-speed by horns, trumpets and trombones, once more the wind and upper strings skip through their mocking dance. (It is worth mentioning that the bells continue their seemingly random chime regardless of the length or natural stress of the phrases beneath.) With each new stanza of the Dies Irae, Berlioz introduces striking additions to the score, their effectiveness being the greater for their stark simplicity. For example, strange grunts from cellos and basses pant after the theme a quaver late, while the bass drum hammers remorselessly at the second beat of the bar. The effect is curiously unstable so that our rhythmic sense becomes disoriented. At last, after a number of chaotic false starts, the Witches' Round Dance gets under way.

Surprisingly, in so scandalous a context, it turns out to be a fugue of sorts, too respectable a form, one might think, for such an occasion. However, its progress is disrupted from time to time by blasphemously syncopated 'Amens' from the brass. The strings carry the burden of the fugal exposition with bustling counterpoints giving a hectic quality that avoids the taint of academicism. Soon the fugal structure disintegrates in a scatter of chromatic scales followed by a strange wailing, alternately loud and soft.

117

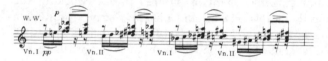

There is no harmony here, no attempt to soften the impact of these stark unisons which extend across three octaves (bassoon to piccolo). It is worth remembering that the symphony was first performed five years after Beethoven's death and eight years before Tchaikovsky was even born. It is hardly surprising that critical opinion has often been hostile to Berlioz; the man who flies in the face of convention is not welcome at everyone's table. By starting the Round Dance as a fugue and then continuing in so unorthodox a manner Berlioz was inviting criticism from every pedant who could churn out fugues to a text-book formula. We today should be more perceptive and realize that he was exhibiting a daring comparable to that of Stravinsky in *The Rite of Spring*.

As the movement develops we find the exploitation of extreme contrasts increases, shattering blasts on the full brass section sending the woodwind flying for cover. The suggestion of wings is conveyed with this figuration:

the whispering lift of the pinions in the violins and the downward beat of the wings in the woodwind chords are brilliantly descriptive. The final 'flight' places the wind chords *on* the beat with a softly whirring trill on the first violins, while second violins and violas shadow the woodwind following a quaver later, their dry pizzicato suggesting the sharp claws at the tip of a bat's wing. Gradually suppressed in volume, the music grows increasingly mysterious; violins and violas provide a subdued tremolando in closely-knit harmony while the lower strings and bassoons pursue each other through a sequence of diminished seventh arpeggios. Occasionally a single note will stab through the texture from a solo horn, sounding astonishingly like bells. The Dies Irae theme reappears on a solo cello doubled by horns, who ingeniously divide the notes between them so that all are present and correct. Chromatic murmurings from two solo violas suggest the wind moaning through the ruins of the church. It is spine-tingling stuff, a descent into darkness that has the stench of evil about it. The lowest point is reached with a roll on the bass drum; gradually, in ever-rising sequences the strings move towards the huge climax, their ascent from the nether regions being signalled from time to time by stabbing notes from a horn or restless syncopations from woodwind and horns in consort. At the peak of the climb we find four tremendous bars in which the bulk of the orchestra – woodwind, two horns, two cornets and all the strings – plays consistently after the beat giving us an impression of terrifying insecurity. The heavy brass aided by timpani endeavour to restore order by punching out no less than thirteen chords *on* the beat, generating a sense of conflict that is quite remarkable. (Incidentally notice the extraordinary effectiveness of a single piccolo adding its shrill dissenting voice after the brass entry.) Despite this period of chaos, order is restored as the strings in unison reintroduce the fugue subject.

At this point Berlioz pulls off a feat of composition of which he was clearly proud since he points it out on the score for those too thick-headed to realize what is happening. *Dies Irae et Ronde du Sabbat* he proclaims, and indeed the two are briefly combined, brass and wind belting out the Dies Irae while the strings provide a nimble counterpoint based on the fugal theme of the Round Dance. It is a musical jigsaw that cannot be made to fit for long and Berlioz is soon compelled to resort to fairly conventional running figuration of a type that will fit against most things. As the great plainsong chant reaches its close the strings are left virtually on their own, the second violins being given urgent syncopations that have an air of desperation about them. They lead to a powerful reiteration of the dominant of A minor, treated in an almost pointillist fashion, so rapidly are the chords divided between strings and wind. Suddenly the sound seems to break off, leaving an eerie twittering effect that must have staggered audiences of the day. The violins and violas are asked to play *col legno*, with the wood of the bow, bouncing it off the string in a drum-like rhythm. The discrepancy between what we hear and what we see on the score is intriguing, for Berlioz devises an interlocking system of rhythms that in conjunction produce this pattern:

No instrument actually plays this, but an examination of the three different rhythms shown below will show how the illusion is created.

Spiky, brittle and transparent, it is a texture that might illustrate a Paul Klee painting, so 'modern' does it seem. Once this rhythmic background is established, the woodwind in unison introduce a new version of the fugal Round Dance, now in a minor key and pointed with venomous trills. Cellos and basses provide a light-footed dancing bass, pizzicato. The three sections involved, woodwind, upper strings and lower strings, are completely independent of each other, each pursuing a different course, the balance being so expertly contrived that the ear can disentangle precisely what is happening.

119

The same can scarcely be said of the passage that follows immediately after, a musical shower of sparks from staccato wind whose rapid shifts of harmony baffle the ear. All those who are anti-Schoenberg and who find the twelve-note system of composition anathema would do well to ponder this clarinet part.

As can be seen, all twelve notes of the chromatic scale are used within a very brief space of time. This in itself might not be all that remarkable were it not for the fact that the flute, oboe and bassoon parts show a corresponding angularity while also touching on all the available chromatic notes, albeit in dissimilar patterns. The passage is truly prophetic, if unwittingly so, and it is hardly surprising that the full brass section is called upon to restore some harmonic stability with three massive chords, each evoking a well-nigh hysterical screech from the woodwind. A weird convulsive tremolando from the strings momentarily diverts us from the key of C towards which we are supposedly heading, but the brass have suffered enough procrastination and with a tremendous dominant seventh (complete with the thunder of two timpani) bring us back on course.

One would imagine that the fertility of Berlioz's invention would have withered by this stage, but the Coda on which he now embarks proves to be full of ingenious new touches. For example the two tubas set out on a three-steps-at-a-time version of the scale of C major, a rather boring cliché if ever there was one.

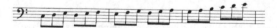

Now most composers would either double this on the strings or reinforce the first note of each group with suitable harmonies. Berlioz writes string parts that only he could have conceived, compact little fragments that relate to the pattern in the tubas but whose rapid flicks are like a jockey's whip urging his mount along the final straight. (See page 121.)

This passage builds to a peak of excitement before plunging into one of the strangest episodes of the whole symphony. For the last time the tubas recall the opening notes of the Dies Irae. No longer starkly unaccompanied, they are backed by music which suggests the convulsions of a man racked by fever. It is not the harmonies that are strange but the dynamics; bass drum and strings share the same extraordinary alternations.

120

(The crescendo and diminuendo are only indicated in the first bar of the drum part but may logically be expected to continue.) It is probably safe to say that nowhere else in all music is there a comparable example of extreme and concentrated dynamic contrasts. The effect is neurotic to the point of madness, calculated to leave an audience literally gasping. Emerging from this final nightmare, the music gallops away in a last sprint for home, the two timpanists heightening the excitement with some virtuoso drumming. Notice how a single piccolo and E flat clarinet can make their shrill voices heard above a full orchestra; notice too the effectiveness of the pounding chromatic descents in trombones and tuba. The purist may flinch, regarding these closing pages as coarse and vulgar, yet one cannot deny the overwhelming impact of the sound. In the very final bar Berlioz added a cymbal clash, a last extravagant gesture that is doomed to be drowned in a storm of applause.

Berlioz: Symphonie Fantastique

It has taken a long time for the genius of Berlioz to be fully recognized. Those who regard him as a musical megalomaniac forget how frequently he exercises an extraordinary economy in his writing. In the slow movement of this very symphony there is a long expressive melody scored for violins and flute virtually without accompaniment. Not one of his contemporaries would have taken such a risk; indeed it is his sheer daring in orchestration that is so exhilarating. In the Romeo and Juliet Symphony there is a scene when Romeo comes to Juliet's tomb, and finding her apparently lifeless body, loses his reason. I doubt if in all nineteenth-century music one could find a more courageously experimental passage for orchestra. Berlioz himself could never have heard anything like it; he had no model to base his technique upon. Yet despite the perpetual discouragement of under-rehearsed insecure performances, he persisted in finding his own path. To fully understand such a man one must identify oneself with his aspirations, share his dreams. Fortunately he made this easy for us by writing the most entertaining autobiography ever penned by a musician.[1] Within its pages one can find all the clues one needs to comprehend his totally individual style. I am prepared to admit that had the Symphonie Fantastique been composed some fifty years later I might not regard it with quite such astonishment. Placed in the context of the early 1830s, it must surely be acknowledged as one of the supremely original works of all time, original in conception and original in execution.

[1] *Memoirs of Hector Berlioz.* Trans. and ed. David Cairns.

11

Tchaikovsky
Romeo and Juliet *Overture-fantasy*

Piccolo
2 Flutes
2 Oboes
2 Clarinets
Cor Anglais
2 Bassoons

4 Horns
2 Trumpets
3 Trombones
Tuba

Harp

Timpani
Bass Drum
Cymbals

Strings

Although the sequence of musical events bears little relationship to the play, this famous overture contains a number of themes which are clearly identifiable, whether as characters such as Friar Laurence or the Nurse, or as concepts such as Love or the feud between the Montagues and Capulets. As one might expect, musical characterization of this sort is greatly helped by orchestration, a blend of woodwind giving an organ-like quality to the Friar's theme, muted strings conveying the tender affection the Nurse feels for Juliet, the heavy brass and percussion adding drama to the duels and street-fights.

The opening phrases are scored for woodwind quartet (two clarinets, two bassoons). The clarinets are kept low, the second player's part consistently lying below the first bassoon. This technique of dove-tailing produces a sombre blend of tone-colour that is typical of Tchaikovsky. While the suggestion of an organ is certainly intended, the music also conveys premonitions of tragedy, a feeling that is confirmed by the first lamenting phrases we hear from the strings. The pressure-points in the harmony as the strings first enter are not all that unlike the tensions that Wagner used in the opening bars of *Tristan und Isolde*. Both composers knew how to exploit chromatic dissonances. However, Tchaikovsky resists the temptation to wallow in grief so early in the work, and in bar 21 embarks on a passage of great tenderness. Once more the wind parts (flutes and clarinets now) are beautifully interwoven as they begin their gradual ascent to a widely spaced chord of F minor. They are helped on their way by a chain of thirds from divided cellos. It is interesting at such moments to imagine alternative scoring. Suppose for instance that the flute and clarinet parts had been given to the first and second violins, and that the sequence of thirds were to be played by two clarinets instead of the cellos. As orchestration, such a lay-out would be perfectly acceptable; indeed it would be a more orthodox solution. What are the arguments against it?

Having just given the strings two phrases that are laden with grief, it would be unconvincing, even illogical, instantly to change their role to that of comforter. Moreover, having established the organ-like tones of the wind to symbolize Friar Laurence, Tchaikovsky not unnaturally wishes to sustain the convention. As for the possible substitution of clarinets for cellos, they could not bring as much richness to the harmonically interesting inner parts as the cellos do. By giving the melodic line to the wind, Tchaikovsky preserves a certain classical detachment, holding plenty in reserve against later events. Similarly, had he scored the opening bars for divided violas and cellos, the sound would already have been too essentially romantic in character, defeating the poignancy of the subsequent string entry.

I have already mentioned the F minor chord to which this ascending phrase has been leading. It is scored in a most intriguing way so as to convey a curious bleakness.

At the top of the chord we find flutes and clarinets interlocked, each pair of instruments playing an octave.

A long way beneath them, the cor anglais and the two bassoons sustain the bass note.

The gulf between these extremes is filled by the four horns.

Of the strings, only the violas and double basses have anything to contribute at this stage.

The scoring is deliberately planned so as to give a feeling of emptiness, as though one were standing in the vast deserted ballroom of an Italian ducal palace. Having created this space, Tchaikovsky proceeds to fill it with a rising sequence of seven chords on the harp, a balletic gesture which gives some support to my notion that he visualized the ballroom where Romeo caught his first sight of Juliet, a ballroom now filled with ghosts rather than colourfully dressed dancers. The gesture is made twice more, the only change of colour being the addition of cellos to enrich the bass. The exhortation *ppp* has a touch of wishful thinking about it since the flautist has not been born who can play a top A flat really quietly.

Now those who remember the play's violent opening may question Tchaikovsky's decision to begin his overture so sombrely. After all, did not Shakespeare grip his audience's attention with a street brawl between the feuding families and their retinues? ('What, ho! you men, you beasts, that quench the fire of your pernicious rage with purple fountains issuing from your veins . . .') I am convinced that Tchaikovsky imagined that the tale was being told by Friar Laurence, hence the emphasis on his music in the opening pages. He may even have seen a production in which the Prologue was spoken by the Friar.

With those wide-spaced chords the Friar leads us through the deserted palaces, soon, as the story unfolds, to be peopled in our imagination by the characters of the play. I proffer this interpretation simply because I was for a long time baffled by the section which now ensues. It is begun by the strings who, in unison, play small groups of three notes at a time (pizzicato), gradually accumulating into longer scale-like passages. Meanwhile, starting in the fourth bar of the strings, the woodwind begin a more positive version of the very opening theme, the one that both in its ecclesiastical tone and organ-like scoring has surely identified itself as the Friar. Yet this same theme is destined at a later point to play a prominent part in the most hectic battle scenes, when, according to the listener's preference, it can serve equally well to represent Romeo, Tybalt or simply the Feud.

If, however, we regard Friar Laurence as the narrator of a story that came to its tragic ending some time ago, this enigmatic section begins to make sense. With those pizzicato notes the characters literally begin to come to life – again a balletic conception. As he warms to his tale the figures grow more vivid in our minds, beginning once more to inhabit the long empty corridors, the courts and terraces. 'My story is of a feud between two noble families,' the Friar tells us. 'It all began here in this very building, but who was to know it would come to such a tragic end . . .' He pauses to sigh at the memory, a sigh we hear eloquently expressed on the strings (bars 52–60). In adopting this interpretation I have to revise my former conception of the very opening bars. They do not represent Friar Laurence himself but the Voice of Friar Laurence playing the part of Prologue.

While this may be dismissed as pure speculation, having little to do with orchestration, I would defend myself by saying that every idea I have put forward about the 'meaning' of the music has been prompted entirely by a detailed study of the score. There is an old adage which says, 'Ask no questions and you'll be told no lies'; but if we ask no questions, we will never learn the truth, and the question, 'Why did Tchaikovsky begin this overture with over 100 bars of slow music?' is worth asking. On the other hand I am well aware of the danger of searching for literal interpretations of programmatic music since the demands of musical structure frequently over-ride the logical continuity of a story.

Such is the case now, when, for purely musical reasons, Tchaikovsky repeats (albeit in a different key) the entire section contained between bars 21–37. The orchestration this time is notably warmer; violins do take over the sustained lines originally given to flutes and clarinets; the chains of thirds once played by divided cellos alone are now scored for oboes, bassoons and violas. The culminating chord (E minor instead of F minor) is quite differently spaced.

Admittedly there is still a space for the harp to fill with its seven spread chords, but notice how much more reticent are the shriller-voiced woodwind, now replaced by the more lyrical strings. The whole feel of the phrase has changed; it is softer, more veiled.

Beneath the final chord of this section a soft timpani roll begins, injecting a note of menace. At once tension spreads through the strings, the sort of phrase that would have a ballerina wringing her hands in anguish. It is interesting to notice how alternations between strings and wind, which up to now have been relatively leisurely, are suddenly tautened, so that the wind will pick on just two notes from a string phrase. It is an ingenious way of changing the time-scale. Gathering pace the music moves on to the first Allegro, propelled on its way by a horn part that would have been impracticable at the time of the *Symphonie Fantastique*.

Such passages make one realize the immense gain that came with the invention of valved horns, able to play a full chromatic scale instead of being limited to the harmonic series.

Quite a sharp dialogue follows – the first intimation of the hostilities that break out whenever Montague meets Capulet. The entire wind section in unison (piccolo and cor anglais included) are pitted against two horns supported by the violas. One might expect such a contest to be unequal but it proves to be surprisingly well matched, partly because the tone colours of the opposed forces are so different. The music is interrupted by a thunderous roll on the timpani. (Is Tchaikovsky making a brief reference to the opening scene of the play when the Prince of Verona angrily quells the riot?) The rumble of the timpani dies away and once more we hear the sighing phrase from the strings already referred to on pages 124 and 126. It is given new significance as Tchaikovsky reveals its relationship to the hostile exchange that immediately precedes it:

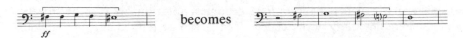

For seven bars there is a strange alternation of wind and string chords like two fencers squaring up to each other; the harmony is completely static, creating the feeling that something *must* break loose.

It does. Without more ado we are pitched into the first 'fight scene' with full wind reinforced by horns, strings and timpani. The dense harmony and powerfully syncopated rhythms suggest that more than two protagonists are involved, yet there are passages when Tchaikovsky seems to have a clear image of two swordsmen in mind. Upward scales in the violins, downward scales in violas and cellos vividly convey the forward lunge and thrust on one side, the deft retreat and parry on the other.

Notice how in the third bar of the example above the second violins take theme; suppressed though it is at this stage its rhythmic vitality makes a

127

century fashion, Firsts on the conductor's left, Seconds on his right, the sense of conflict would have been heightened by such a cross-over. Stereophonic effects are not a twentieth century innovation!

As the fight sequence proceeds it becomes somewhat more stylized – a bar of strings, a bar of wind, a bar of strings, a bar of wind. Certainly it is a duel of orchestral sonorities but a little too tidy to be totally convincing. Compositional technique takes command as Tchaikovsky initiates a canon between the lower strings and the upper wind. Scurrying figuration from the violins adds excitement of a sort, but I have always felt in performance that this section is constructed to too pat a formula. As though aware that the rhythms have become a shade too predictable, Tchaikovsky plunges us into the most exciting passage in the whole work. The strings begin a rapid unison run spread over eight bars and covering a range of two and a half octaves. (Note that the double basses are judged to be incapable of staying the pace for more than a bar and a half.) Against this torrent of notes, the full wind section, horns, trumpets, timpani and cymbals have a series of violent chords so irregularly spaced that they have become a notorious trap for the unwary. The unpredictability of the chord placings can be judged at a glance when shown against the regular four beats in each bar.

One might argue that this is taking artistic licence too far since these tremendous clashes suggest giants in armour fighting with broadswords rather than nimble-footed Italians slashing with rapiers and daggers, but the effect is so overwhelming that criticism is stilled. Moreover Tchaikovsky has enough restraint to hold his trombones, tuba and bass drum in reserve for one last monumental blow before battle is joined again with renewed vigour. The precise placing of the cymbal clashes reveals the care with which Tchaikovsky would orchestrate even the loudest passages, since for the most part they are slotted in at the exact moment where the remainder of the orchestra has a quaver rest.

Gradually the tumult dies; clarinet and flute exchange brief phrases which are duly taken up and extended by a solo bassoon until at last there is little left save a low grumble from cellos and basses with occasional bell-like chords from a trio of horns. There is an air of expectancy that could be sensed even by someone who had never heard the work before. The 'event', once it happens, is worth the wait. For twenty bars the bass has lingered on the note A as an implied dominant of D major. With a masterly avoidance of the obvious, Tchaikovsky lets it slip down a semitone to A flat, thus opening the door to the totally unexpected key of D *flat* major. For the first time we are given a taste of the Love Theme which, needless to say, has in recent years been hacked out of context and sacrificed on the altar of Commercialism. (The fact that Tchaikovsky himself made it into an aria for Romeo in an abortive attempt to write an operatic treatment of the story in no way excuses the vulgarizations which have been perpetrated by 'arrangers' on the dubious pretext of bringing Art to the Masses.) That the theme stands for Romeo rather than the abstract conception of Love is made clear by its initial orchestration. Cor anglais and violas in unison are a reasonable orchestral substitute for the tenor voice; indeed in one period of history the violas were known as 'tenor fiddles'.

With considerable self-control Tchaikovsky refrains from developing the tune at its first appearance, just the first eight bars being all we are allowed. There follows an enchanting passage for muted violins over a drone bass in the violas. The phrase rocks gently to and fro with subtle chromaticisms disguising its essential simplicity. There can be no doubt that the music portrays the Nurse, the drone bass confirming her peasant origin. Gradually the web of harmonies extends until the strings are divided into eight parts. A rising scale on flute and oboe suggests Juliet's flying feet as she rushes like an eager child to greet her lover. This time the tune is extended to its full length.

The scoring of this first full version is notably free from sentimentality; flutes and oboes in unison can scarcely be called lush, while the strings are confined to pure accompaniment. The stroke of genius is the solo horn playing a long sequence of paired notes that are like a passionate lover's caress. It is a moment every audience waits for; without it, the tune in this version would sound somewhat undernourished. As a symbol of the ardour of young love the horn part could scarcely be bettered, and yet, compared to the sumptuous extravagances of Richard Strauss, it is simplicity itself.

As the long and expressive tune comes to its conclusion the harp picks up the idea of paired crotchets from the solo horn, amplifying them into chords of six notes. The strings, still muted, provide a soft cushion of sustained harmony while occasional brief phrases from a bassoon offer some melodic interest. The harp chords gradually descend from the upper register; at the ninth bar of this passage Tchaikovsky initiates a touching duet between bassoon and cor anglais.

On the note marked with a *sfz* the double basses add a single vibrant pizzicato that effectively underlines the unexpected B double-flat. It is such attention to small detail that shows how fastidious was Tchaikovsky's imaginative ear. As the strings drop out they are replaced by a dark-hued chord for woodwind, unusually laid out with the cor anglais above the clarinets, a bassoon below them. The harp part drifts into silence until at last the music is reduced to a single note on the violas. Just at the moment when it

129

seems to have lost all momentum Tchaikovsky reintroduces the Feud theme; suppressed though it is at this stage its rhythmic vitality makes a strong contrast to the expansive and lyrical music which we have just experienced. The conflict between strings and woodwind is renewed.

Tchaikovsky's purpose here is to convey the tension that lurks beneath the surface in Verona since the Prince issued his edict forbidding any further hostilities between the two rival houses of Montague and Capulet. The dynamic level of the music is for the most part kept down to *p* or *pp*; even those phrases that are clearly meant to represent running feet are kept to a furtive scurry. As is often the case the simplest device is the most effective. For as much as nine bars at a time the violins will fidget restlessly on the same note while trombones and trumpets exchange terse phrases with the woodwind. The suggestion of reluctantly suppressed antagonism is brilliantly conveyed. From time to time horns or wind will measure out the theme from the very opening bars of the work but in the more positive version we have come to associate with the feud. Suddenly the tension flares into action as cellos and basses launch an attack:

To begin the second fight sequence thus with only a single strand of orchestral sound leaves the composer with huge reserves. They are skilfully brought into play, with hurrying scales in the first violins suggesting reinforcements rushing to join in the fray. A cymbal clash coupled with a strident trumpet entry tells us that battle has been joined. Now while Tchaikovsky frequently uses a technique of Action and Reaction – trombones following trumpets half a bar behind, violins following cellos a mere beat behind – there comes a moment when everyone must accept the trumpets' lead. In brazen splendour they proclaim the theme of the Feud:

(Again note that such a trumpet part would not have been practicable in Mozart's, Haydn's or Beethoven's day; it can be played only on a valved instrument.) They and they alone play *on* the beat; the whole of the rest of the orchestra hammers out this rhythm ♪♫ on the second and fourth beats of each bar, save only the bass drum who must be content with a single massive blow on the off beats. If this seems like unfair discrimination against the drummer, it is worth pointing out that he can make more sound with an explosive single crotchet than he can with a triple repeated note. After eight glorious bars even the trumpets are thrown off the beat and the phrase opens out with the brass progressing in contrary motion towards a reprise of the sword-clashing climax already described on p. 128. For several pages the battle rages exactly as before, a gesture towards a conventional symphonic recapitulation that Tchaikovsky considers to be of structural value. Only in its final two bars does it change direction when the strings are given a precipitate scale that plunges down to D through two and a half octaves. The excitement is instantly quelled as they settle into a gently murmuring figuration above which the two oboes and a single clarinet recall the Nurse's theme.

Tchaikovsky's treatment of this potentially boring accompaniment is typical of his ingenuity. The basic material is this simple pattern repeated (with occasional slight variants) for some nineteen bars.

How easily this could degenerate into a repetitious finger exercise of the sort that students are only too thankful to leave behind them for ever; instead, Tchaikovsky keeps the players constantly alert by distributing segments of the pattern alternately to first and second violins.

To give this unbroken continuity undisturbed by involuntary accents demands real concentration.

Little by little Tchaikovsky adds to the texture, bringing in first a discreet enrichment of the bass with cellos and bassoon, next the cor anglais moving in parallel with another bassoon, then a flute, followed two bars later by the third horn. Meanwhile the woodwind harmonies extend their range step by step just as the muted strings had done nearly two hundred bars earlier. In the strings the semiquaver figuration continues, though it too begins to reach out over a wider compass. The entry of the harp is a signal to break free from these limitations; a majestic rising scale, suggesting the great curtains of a theatre opening to reveal a scene of matchless splendour, leads us to the impassioned reprise we have all been waiting for.

We now see how wise Tchaikovsky was to have held his strings in reserve for this memorable climax. Instead of flutes and oboes with a gentle murmur of strings in the background, he now gives us the richness of violins, violas and cellos in unison pouring their collective hearts out as this truly operatic melody unfolds. A single piccolo adds a silver streak to the violin tone; the rest of the woodwind are given throbbing harmonies, twelve repeated notes to each bar, while the impassioned horn part is now given to two players instead of one. Since the cellos are fully occupied with the tune, the double basses need some support and this is tactfully provided by the two bassoons

131

(an octave higher) and the tuba (at the same pitch). A timpani roll helps to build the tune towards its ultimate climax, at which point trombones and trumpets are brought in to overwhelming effect. Having attained this supreme moment, the music begins to fade, giving Tchaikovsky the opportunity to display characteristic sensitivity. The play is a tragedy; the lovers' ecstasy is denied them by cruel circumstance. The point is made clear in one of the most beautiful passages in the whole overture.

The cellos, no doubt encouraged by the instruction *amoroso*, lead off with a poignantly distorted version of the theme accompanied by delicately poised groups of six notes to a beat in violins and violas – Juliet's fluttering heart perhaps? The phrase is partially echoed by flutes and oboe in unison while clarinets and cor anglais sustain a central core of harmony. The exchange between cellos and woodwind takes place a second time with increased intensity. Then, to magnificently heroic effect, the cellos are supplanted by the four horns in unison. They in turn are echoed by the upper woodwind, whereupon the trombones and tuba add their massive weight to the harmony in preparation for one last impassioned version of the lovers' theme.

At this point Tchaikovsky was presented with an intriguing problem. He needed the timpani to build a crescendo of sufficient intensity. The proper bass to the harmony is A, powerfully reiterated by trombone and tuba, second bassoon and double basses. Given adequate time, it would have been practical enough for the timpanist to tune the B kettledrum down a tone to A; unfortunately Tchaikovsky required the B a few bars later. With modern pedal timpani such changes are managed with ease, but with the old-fashioned screw adjustments a change of even a tone would have taken too long to allow accurate re-tuning. We therefore find in interesting discrepancy between the actual bass (A) and the enforced B on the timpani. Happily the harmony makes this clash acceptable since the essential chord consists of the notes A, B, D sharp and F sharp in ascending order. The resolution of this harmony onto a chord of E major provides a neat solution, the timpanist's B serving as a pivot between the two harmonies.

The musical symbolism before the final coda may be interpreted in more than one way. For one last time the combined strings try to re-establish the lovers' theme but before even two bars have been completed the whole woodwind section in unison make a passionate reply.

The simple explanation is to see this in operatic terms, the strings standing for Romeo, the wind supplying Juliet's despairing response. Remembering, though, that in all the 'fight' sequences hostility between the two families has been represented by rapid alternations of strings and woodwind, it could well be that the deeper meaning of this passage is that this 'pair of star-cross'd lovers' are doomed to be perpetually separated, that strings and wind are, *sua generis*, incompatible. From now on, interruptions from the 'conflict' motif become increasingly frequent, try though the strings may to preserve the lyrical strain. A magnificent new development of the very opening theme of the work appears. It has served as the voice of the Friar, it has served as a continuing thread through the scenes of conflict; now it must surely stand for Fate, if not for Death itself. Scored for full brass with the bassoons, oboes, cor anglais and bottom strings adding all the additional weight they can, it strides on remorselessly while violins, violas and the shriller woodwind appear to fly in panic. The music grows increasingly frenzied, the alternations between strings and brass more rapid. One could argue that in relation to the play the proportions have got completely out of scale. This is no duel between Tybalt and Mercutio nor even Romeo's swift revenge; it is a battle between armies at the least. Tchaikovsky's imagination has taken him far beyond the confines of a stage or of Verona itself; he has become intoxicated with the sheer power of orchestral sound which makes even Shakespeare's heroes seem puny by comparison. Nevertheless he clearly has a sword-fight in mind at the loudest point of the entire work (bars 467–71) as the frequent cymbal clashes indicate. To ask which sword-fight is irrelevant since, apart from the slaying of Paris in the tomb, all the duelling is over by Act III, Scene 1 with nearly half the play still to be enacted. Tchaikovsky justifiably calls the Overture a Fantasy, granting himself full artistic licence to juggle events as he pleases. The whole conception of the closing minutes of the work is concerned with the portrayal of heroic figures caught up in violent and tragic events; the music would serve as well for a dozen plays.

The 'fight' music, having reached its ferocious climax, gradually disintegrates into briefer phrases, though losing little of its force. Isolated notes on the trombones make a notable effect, heavy with a sense of impending doom; at last only cellos, basses and bassoons are left, their final note being drowned by a shattering roll on the timpani. There is a silence. Wholly different in mood from anything that has gone before, the Coda begins. It is a funeral march of sorts, as the measured drum-beat and the deep pizzicato of the double-basses reveal. Violins, cellos and a solo bassoon offer us a distorted fragment of the lovers' theme, the cellos serving to darken the violin tone. Darker still is the second phrase, violas and cellos pulling the theme into the shadows. The music seems about to die away to oblivion when suddenly and unexpectedly Tchaikovsky introduces a sort of benediction, scored for the full woodwind choir. (Horns are included as a liaison between the bassoons and cor anglais.) It is a model of scoring for wind though demanding perfection of intonation and perfectly synchronized breathing. As its final Amen sounds, the harp has a rising sequence of chords that seems to waft the souls of the dead lovers heavenwards. Cynics may dismiss the conception as Hollywood at its worst, but Tchaikovsky is master enough to bring it off. The sixteen bars of wind tone serve to banish all suggestion of sentimentality. Their effect is to cleanse the ear so that when the violins re-enter on a high B the quality is truly ethereal by contrast. Three times the unison strings remind us of the opening fragment of the lovers' theme but restless syncopations in the wind parts prevent the music from becoming self-indulgent in its expression of grief. To our surprise a drum-roll begins, growing in volume so that the last vestiges of sentiment are driven away as though by some monstrous tremor of the earth. Hard and implacable, eight tremendous chords, so irregularly spaced as to be unpredictable in their timing, bring the overture to its dramatic and unexpected conclusion. It would be impossible for Tchaikovsky to express more powerfully his determination to eschew sentimentality at all cost. These extraordinary closing bars tell us that the legend of Romeo and Juliet is no boy-and-girl romance but a stark tragedy brought about by the obstinate folly of arrogant families puffed-up with pride; perhaps too they tell us of Tchaikovsky's anger that love should bring such bitterness and sorrow in its wake. It was a subject on which he was qualified to feel strongly.

12

Debussy
Prélude à L'après-midi d'un faune

3 Flutes
2 Oboes
Cor Anglais
2 Clarinets
2 Bassoons

4 Horns

2 Harps

1 Percussion (a pair of 'antique' cymbals)

Strings

This orchestral prelude, which some claim to be the most sensuously beautiful work ever written, represents a totally different approach to the orchestra from anything we have explored so far. Just as the painters of the French Impressionist school were to revolutionize the techniques of applying oil-paint to canvas, so did Debussy change the whole conception of how to orchestrate. Obviously it would be unjust to suggest that he alone was responsible for the fundamental change of attitude; other composers such as Delius or Skryabin were also attempting successfully to escape from the all-prevading influence of Wagner which threatened to swamp music in the closing decade of the nineteenth century. While Richard Strauss, Bruckner and Mahler endeavoured in their individual ways to *extend* the Wagnerian concept of Germanic Romanticism, those who fought against the tide could be divided into several camps. For some, folk-music seemed to offer an escape from emotional excess, whether in the pastoral lyricism of Vaughan Williams or the irregular metre and acerbic harmonies of Bartók. For others a more cerebral solution seemed to be called for, the neo-classicism of Hindemith and (later) Stravinsky, or the fundamentally new musical syntax known as Serialism, devised by Schoenberg. None of these alternatives held any attraction for Debussy. From childhood onwards he had been fascinated by the spell of exotic harmony, individual collective sounds that avoided any association with a specific key-centre. One does not so much hear Debussy harmonies as savour them, each sound being beauti-

135

ful in its own right. Many, but by no means all, are based on the whole-tone scale, a six-note scale that has no fixed tonality. Chords built up from this scale are elusive in quality, lacking any firm commitment to conventional keys such as A major or B minor. Although this work has a key-signature of four sharps and even finishes with a chord of E major, it cannot really be said to be *in* E, the signature being one of convenience rather then identity.

Taking a poem by Stéphane Mallarmé as his inspiration, Debussy originally planned to write a three-movement suite consisting of a Prelude, Interlude and Paraphrase Finale. An advance announcement of this orchestral triptych was even printed by his publishers in 1893, but in the event only the Prelude was ever completed. It was Debussy's first purely orchestral work, his entries for the coveted Prix de Rome being of necessity for voices and orchestra. Apart from the set compositions demanded of the advanced students at the Conservatoire he had composed a few songs and piano pieces, a string quartet and a setting of Sarrazin's French translation of Rossetti's poem 'The Blessed Damozel' which was published in a limited edition of a hundred and sixty copies in 1893 under the title *La Demoiselle Élue*. A *Fantaisie* for piano and orchestra was supposed to have been played at one of the concerts of the Société Nationale in April 1890, but at the penultimate rehearsal Debussy calmly gathered up the orchestral parts from the stands and withdrew the work; it was not to be performed again until after his death.

Like most of his fellow-students, Debussy passed through a fanatically pro-Wagnerian phase, poring for hours over the score of *Tristan* in particular. During his mid-twenties he began to realize the potential danger of so powerful an influence, ultimately proclaiming himself as positively anti-Wagnerian. He began to search for what, in his own phrase, 'came after Wagner's time but not after Wagner's manner'. He discovered Maeterlinck's poetic drama *Pelléas et Mélisande* and with considerable courage, together with an ambitious purpose some might have regarded as presumptuous, resolved to make it into an opera which would follow none of the established traditions. It proved to be a labour that was to be spread over a number of years, with the constant revision and drastic rewriting that indicate how severe a critic he was of his own creations. With such a major enterprise in the forefront of his mind it is hardly surprising that the symphonic triptych based on the Mallarmé poem should have become less important to him; yet it was not Debussy's custom to allow any work to be performed until he was totally satisfied that it measured up to his standards of individual perfection. The single movement that was completed was subjected to a number of carefully considered revisions which even continued into the orchestral rehearsals under the conductor Gustave Doret. The official first performance was given on Saturday, 22 December 1894. Debussy was then thirty-two. To his delight the second performance followed immediately afterwards – such was the applause that the work was repeated. For Debussy, who had fallen somewhat foul of the French musical establishment, this was a truly heartening encouragement, and it might be argued that the success of *L'après-midi* gave him exactly the support he needed to persevere with the huge task of completing *Pelléas*.

From its very first phrase, *L'après-midi* seems to enter into a new world of tonal experience. The choice of an unaccompanied solo flute to play this languorous chromatic melody miraculously evokes the warm haze of a summer afternoon in a wood where dappled sunlight seen through myriad leaves dazzles the eye. The first harmony we hear is enigmatic (C sharp minor with an added sixth) and is immediately smudged by a delicate harp glissando that seems, like a momentary breeze, to set the leaves rustling. As if itself moved by this gentle zephyr, the harmony subtly shifts to a dominant seventh on B flat, a chord which is quietly confirmed by the second harp and muted strings – violas, cellos and basses divided so as to play a five-note chord. Whether or not he knew Tennyson's line about 'the horns of Elfland faintly blowing', Debussy certainly sensed their magic for we now hear them, exchanging their distant summons across the forest. There is a bar of silence, out of which emerges a subtle echo of the first harmony of the work, no longer scored for the plangent tones of oboes and clarinets but for muted violins. Again the rippling glissando on the harp disturbs the stillness, again the harmony is nudged into its secondary position, the connecting link between two seemingly unrelated chords being the enharmonic relationships between A sharp and B flat.

Once more we hear the distant summons of the horns; it is as though up to this moment we have stood at the very threshold of the forest, still in the clear light of day but gazing into its impenetrable and mysterious depths. Had we the strength of mind, there would still be time to turn away, but when for a second time we hear the hypnotic call of Pan's flute we are drawn irresistibly into the shadows, leaving the everyday world behind us.

A cold analysis of how Debussy achieves this magic shows that this time the flute is not unaccompanied but supported by vaguely shifting harmonies that murmur almost imperceptibly as if in that 'bee-loud glade'. Muted strings play *pp* and tremolando *'sur la touche'*, an instruction which means that the bow should be placed further away from the bridge than normally, over the black ebonite fingerboard, causing the sound to be more veiled and mysterious. A pair of clarinets provide an almost inaudible liaison between the differing tones of the strings and the solo flute.

An oboe takes over the melodic line from the flute (4 bars after Fig. 1) and with its more positive lead encourages more instruments to come in. The shimmering harmonies continue in the lower strings but new colours are added, first a clarinet and then divided first violins to add their support to the oboes while a cor anglais introduces a gently swaying figure that is mirrored by the horns. A particularly subtle piece of scoring places the flutes below the oboes but above (and moving in harmony with) the horns. One might assume it to be an unlikely match but it works amazingly well, the flutes being kept low enough to have a slightly metallic sound which blends perfectly with the horns, particularly when aided by the cor anglais as intermediary. It is a brief surge of fuller tone which quickly dissipates itself with a repeated three-note pattern on a solo clarinet. For the third time the flute begins its haunting melody, this time accompanied not only by a ripple from the harp but by an amazing deep conch-shell note from the horns – something only a genius at orchestration would ever have thought of.

The flute melody is now extended with delightful caprice, the metric pulse alternating between 12/8 and 9/8 to avoid the slightest suggestion of rigidity. The accompaniment remains subdued, with shadowy strings and flecks of sunlight on the harp. Showing a completely practical consideration for his player (who being mortal does have to breathe from time to time), Debussy allows the second flute to take over for the duration of one full beat; if we are tempted to interpret this as the arrival of the playmate for our Pan-like protagonist, we are quickly corrected as the two flutes continue in perfect unison. Perhaps a newcomer is about to arrive, but not until the next phrase.

The change of character is sharply defined; the new solo voice is a clarinet, the tone made sinister by the addition of a shock chord on muted horns. Immediately there is a strangely urgent reaction in the cellos. No longer muted, they have a swift drum-like repetition of one note followed by a brief sinuous undulation. It is a sound that one feels must have been prompted by some image drawn from nature, the drumming feet of a rabbit perhaps, signalling danger, the twitching of a deer's tail, or even the staccato beat of a woodpecker. Since it is always preceded by the stabbing dissonance on the horns, it seems most likely that it is indicative of fear, whether it be the swift patter of feet or the sudden quickening of a tiny pulse. The suggestion is confirmed by some unmistakable 'hops' in the harp part and quite marked pizzicato chords that give the impression of just such springing leaps as a deer makes. Without wishing to introduce too Disneyish an element into the music, a semblance of a plot appears. Is it possible that the sudden change of timbre from flute to clarinet and the 'alert' chord on the horns signify that our faun has sighted a female, and that the 'fear' reaction from the cellos followed by the characteristic leaps for cover are meant to portray the female's response to an imminent assault? The idea is not too far-fetched although, since Debussy did not have a ballet in mind when he wrote it, it becomes dangerously anthropomorphic to assume that the ensuing lyrical phrases – *toujours en animant* – necessarily describe the ardour with which the male pursues his conquest. That the music is shamelessly erotic is not in doubt; it is the precise interpretation of that eroticism which is better left to the individual listener's imagination. To have it too accurately charted by a musical analyst could destroy the elusive magic of the piece.

What is undeniable is the appearance of an entirely new theme (Fig. 4) scored initially for a solo oboe but soon to be taken over by the violins and then other wind instruments in rapid interchange. The music is more positive in tone, the supporting harmonies less evanescent. Increasingly the tendency is for the melodic strands to be duplicated whereas in the earlier part of the work almost every significant phrase had been allotted to a solo instrument. Now we find that a flute will be doubled either by a clarinet an octave lower or by an oboe at the same pitch; clarinets and bassoons may double an octave apart or the violas lend their support to an important phrase on the third horn. It should be emphasized that for the most part the melodic units are extremely compact, anything longer than a bar and a half being the exception. After the languor of the opening this gives an impression of greatly heightened impetus, an impression Debussy encourages by his instruction to move on the tempo.

The climax is short-lived. A rotating figure of six quavers circling around three consecutive notes of the scale, three times repeated, brings us back to the original speed (Fig. 6). Skilfully Debussy converts this seemingly not very inspired idea into a hesitant but expressive new theme.

The change of tone-colour at this moment is beautifully calculated, a solo clarinet taking over from two low flutes and harp, while the violins play a descending sequence of four-note chords over a sustained A flat major harmony scored for two bassoons and three horns.

When I was a child I used often to play in some very beautiful gardens not a mile from my home. They were full of wonders, two little square houses woven out of trees, a vast stony grotto with dank mosses and the sound of perpetually dripping water, an underground tunnel, a weird flint-roofed cave where a horse was buried, a dogs' cemetery and avenues of immense trees from distant lands. Some thirty-five years later I revisited them; there was still much to admire, but the further reaches had been allowed to turn into something of a wilderness. I walked to the end of a rhododendron avenue of unnatural beauty and then turned to the right where no path was, picking my way through nettles and long clinging grass. I knew with absolute certainty that I was heading for a special place, some secret and precious sanctuary that I had especially prized all those years ago. Astonishingly I could not remember what it was I was looking for; as surely as if I heard the beckoning call of Pan's flute I had to go on until I found my unknown goal. Suddenly I was upon it, a perfect circle of tall cypress trees, a veritable temple in the forest with a small marble *prie-dieu* in the centre with a cracked and fading inscription on it. This had been my childhood chapel, infinitely more significant to me than any church or cathedral. It had lost none of its magic even though two trees had lost their strength and were leaning on their neighbours for support. The coronet of the tree-tops, now drawn more closely together, focussed one's gaze upon the sky; the slight movement of the boughs, all pointing heavenwards, made a gentle whisper that sounded like perpetual prayer. I am not drawn to orthodox religion but if ever I felt the need to seek out God that is where I would be most hopeful of finding him.

The relevance of this to Debussy's symphonic prelude may seem absurdly remote but at its heart (p. 15 out of 31) we find a passage whose impact is as heart-stopping as was my encounter with that forgotten sanctuary. Despite the basically slow tempo, every melodic fragment has moved with sinuous grace and flexibility; the movement has been consistently supple. Now – and our arrival at it is as unexpected as was mine at my forest temple – we come to a passage of a totally different texture in which we get the impression of halting in wonder before a vista of such beauty that we hold our breath. The key is an unequivocal D flat major, already exquisitely exploited by Debussy in 'Clair de Lune'. The unison woodwind (flutes, oboes, cor anglais and clarinets) suggest not Pan's pipe but an organ, while the barely audible pulsating harmonies in the strings impart an air of such tender sweetness to the sound that even the most hardened orchestral player must feel a pang at its beauty.

Can one describe this as a great melody? Not really, not by any of the hallmarks by which we normally judge the melodic merits of composers as diverse as Mozart, Chopin, Verdi or Puccini. Yet its placing is such that in its context it overwhelms us and this must be partly due to the sheer beauty of the orchestral texture.

For a moment the music seems to lose its way with a twice-repeated falling phrase, to say nothing of a sudden quasi-oriental passage in the wind which Debussy may have unconsciously lifted from Balakirev's *Tamara* which he much admired. Then the D flat phrase quoted above reappears in a completely different orchestral guise. It is the strings who now sustain the melodic line, developing it at some length, even at the cost of substituting passion for a trance-like ecstasy. The change of mood is urged upon them by all the supporting parts which are now restless in cross-accentuation. The harp-parts become busy in figuration subtly reinforcing each other; it is the richest moment of the whole score, yet at no point do we feel that the absence of trumpets, trombones or percussion is in any way a detriment. In this respect it is interesting to compare this central climax with the great final section of *La Mer* (also in D flat major) where Debussy uses the full resources of a large symphony orchestra. In *La Mer* the excitement is continuously augmented until the climactic final chord; in *L'après-midi* the most impassioned section lasts a mere three pages, only to dissolve into gentle murmurings from clarinet or oboe while a solo violin bids a tender farewell to the D flat tune.

And now the strings do quietly establish a firm anchorage in E major, supported by perfectly conventional arpeggio figures from the harp. No longer free as air but placed within the confines of a common time-signature, the flute reminds us of the opening phrase of the work, somewhat modified to conform to the restraints of the sustained E major harmony. Anybody who suspects that this is destined to be a recapitulation of sorts is in for something of a shock since the phrase is scarcely allowed to finish before Debussy introduces a completely new development. The word may be interpreted both dramatically (as a novel episode) and musically (as an ingenious compression of the opening flute theme).

A slightly aggressive oboe presents the substantially quicker, compressed version of the opening motif, its character transformed from indolence to mischief. Once again we find Debussy devising a background that is quite unexpected in tone-colour. Three muted horns set up a quiet swaying motion between these two chords.

The conventional scoring for such a passage would be to put it in the strings, possibly divided violas to give it a special colour. The muted horns make a tangy contrast to the held string chord which has immediately preceded them while at the same time avoiding the slight vagueness and lack of definition which the sound of a body of strings would encourage.

Whatever Debussy imagined to be happening at this moment sparks off a fluttering reaction that suggests a twittering of birds, a brief chirping figure that is passed from flutes to oboes (with cor anglais) and then to clarinets (with bassoon). It is nothing but a quick stir in the forest since the next moment all is calm. Again the strings establish a long sustained harmony – E flat major this time – while, for a change, the oboe imparts a more plaintive note to the initial theme in its restrained version. Another interruption ensues with the cor anglais taking what was previously the oboe's role and more disturbed flutterings from the woodwind. One feels that maybe Puck is about.[1] The general air of restlessness is stilled as two flutes in unison

[1] Besides *L'après-midi d'un faune*, Debussy's works include 'La Danse de Puck', 'Les fées sont d'exquises danseuses', 'La Flute de Pan', *Ondine*, 'Pour invoquer Pan', 'Le tombeau des naiades' and 'Syrinx' – being Pan's last song before his death.

re-establish the opening theme against a shimmering background of string harmony, harmony which now accommodates itself to the chromatic demands of the tune by giving way on the fourth beat of the bar. Two solo violins offer a slightly distorted memory of the clarinet theme quoted on page 139 – a rather touching gesture towards formal orthodoxy on Debussy's part as if to show some doubting soul that these fragments can be co-ordinated into a homogeneous entity. Since the violins immediately embark on a new thematic fragment (supported at a lower octave by a solo cello) the gesture would seem to be wasted. All the same, one does have the feeling that this voyage into an enchanted landscape is coming to its close as the flutes and oboes also offer a reminder of a past event with a triplet figure stolen from the central climax. There is a sense of evening drawing on, brilliantly conveyed by combining the solo flute with a single cello an octave beneath, like a dark shadow. Harmonies sustained on clarinets, bassoons and horns intensify the feeling of approaching darkness, while the gradual slowing of the tempo suggests the sleepy lethargy induced by an afternoon of indolent sensuality in the heat of a summer day. On the very final page, for the only time in the whole work, muted horns and violins present a strangely *harmonized* version of the initial chromatic phrase causing it to seem blurred, out of focus. The percussion player makes his sole contribution with two 'antique' cymbals, a tiny clear bell-like sound that I, perhaps naively, believe to be the first stars appearing in the evening sky. That night is upon us I am certain, for the work ends with two quiet pizzicato chords from cellos and basses.

It was a gentler revolution than that accomplished by Stravinsky with *The Rite of Spring* but not much less significant. In this relatively small-scale work Debussy perfected a new approach to the art of orchestration; if one says that in later and more substantial works he extended his technique, it was more by the use of additional resources than by a change of method. His influence on the language of music was somewhat limited, since whole-tone harmony proved to be incapable of much greater development; to use it was instantly to suggest a pastiche of Debussy. On the other hand, his influence on orchestration was enormous, extending to composers as varied as Stravinsky, Ravel, Szymanowski, Messiaen and many others of lesser stature. Inevitably there came a time when a new generation had to shake off his influence as consciously as he himself had had to banish the ghost of Wagner from his studio. It is to such a composer that I turn for my final example.

13

Britten
Four Sea Interludes from *Peter Grimes*, op. 33a

2 Flutes (both doubling piccolo)
2 Oboes
2 Clarinets
2 Bassoons
Contra-bassoon

4 Horns
3 Trumpets (1 and 2 in C, 3 in D)
3 Trombones
Tuba

Timpani

3 Percussion players (Side Drum, Bass Drum, Cymbals, Gong, Xylophone, Tubular bells, Tambourine)

Harp

Strings

Even the most cursory glance at the list above reveals that while the wind section scarcely differs from that specified by Mozart and Haydn in their later works, and the brass complies with the standard requirements of nineteenth-century composers, it is the percussion section that has been considerably amplified. Even so, Britten's orchestra is modest by twentieth-century standards since the opera was intended to have its première at London's Sadler's Wells Theatre where the pit accommodation is less than one might find at some of the world's larger opera-houses. The point is worth making since a substantial part of the first Interlude is scored for first and second violins in unison, a decision I suspect to have been influenced by the knowledge that the combined strength of both violin sections at Sadlers Wells would scarcely outnumber the normal first violin section of a full symphony orchestra. I can never hear these pieces in a concert-hall without finding the opening phrases too full-bodied in tone. In the original performance there was an ethereal fine-spun quality that was partly caused by a smaller number of players and partly by the boxed-in acoustic of a theatre-pit. For practical and economic reasons, dictated no doubt by printing costs, the omission of the second violins has never been put forward as an option although I would dearly love a conductor to have the courage to try it, even as an experiment in rehearsal. It will of course be argued that Britten himself conducted concert performances of the Sea Interludes and that he could have made the alteration himself. On the other hand, composers tend to be reluctant to make such changes once a work has become established since they may be thought, however unjustly, to be guilty of a loss of confidence.

Interludes or *entr'actes* have long had a classic function to play in opera, whether to show the passage of time, to prepare the mood of the ensuing scene or, more practically, to allow a complex change of scenery to be made. The Sea Interludes are closely integrated into the overall structure of *Peter Grimes* even though they may be enjoyed as orchestral sketches on their own. Their prime interest from the standpoint of orchestral colouring is that each of the four tends to exploit one aspect of orchestral timbre, the first being notably clear and translucent, the second being bright and spiky in tone, the third dark and opaque, the fourth tumultuous and deliberately chaotic. Obviously there are passages of contrast which contradict these generalizations, but just as paintings can differ in intensity of colour according to the way in which the artist has applied his pigment to the canvas, so these four 'tone-paintings' differ substantially in texture.

1 Dawn

Britten lived by or near the sea for most of his life, and many a time as a boy he must have watched the eternally fascinating flight of the gulls with their uncanny ability to hang almost motionless upon the wind, constantly correcting their balance by minute adjustments of their pinions, only to swoop down to the water's surface to gather up some morsel of food and then to climb high again to resume their watching station. Although the first Interlude may be called 'Dawn', I am convinced that the prime image in Britten's mind was the flight of the gull; so it is that the music begins high and clear, unsupported by any harmony, just as the gull itself seems unsupported by any visible force. The flutes (in unison) give a slight edge to the violin tone, preventing it from being merely soft and sweet. The occasional quick 'flick' of two or three notes in the generally slow-moving melodic line may represent wing movements or even the tuneless cry of the gull, but there can be little doubt about the significance of the rippling arpeggio for clarinets, harp and divided violas that suddenly distract our attention from the hovering flight of the bird. It is a scurry of wind across the marshes, setting the reeds rustling and quivering. If I choose marshes rather than a flat expanse of sand at low tide it is because it is through those same marshes that the manhunt for Grimes will be launched near the end of the opera.

Moreover, Aldeburgh has a shingle beach and there is no sandy plain to be seen when the tide is out. . . . The sea is near at hand, though, as the first brass phrase indicates, deep harmonies that suggest a sluggish wave gathering strength lazily, curving its back and subsiding again.

At this point it might be worth making a comparison between the pictorial or descriptive element in this music and Debussy's *L'après-midi*. Both pieces begin with a very evocative and unsupported strand of music, Debussy with a solo flute in its lower compass, Britten with a considerable number of violins and two flutes in a high register. One is vague and nebulous, the other clear and sharply defined. It might seem unnecessarily pejorative in its implications if I were to say that Debussy gives us an Impressionist painting where Britten offers a colour photograph. Colour photographs can be breathtakingly beautiful. Nevertheless there is a marked difference in the approach the two composers have to their self-appointed task of *describing*. Debussy's music is vividly descriptive without a doubt, though doubt may well exist as to precisely what it is descriptive of at any given moment. Most of us are satisfied with such generally agreed concepts as summer heat, haze, woodland, nature, sensuality. We use the word Impressionism since the music deals with impressions rather than substances. Britten's 'line' is as economical as a drawing by Matisse; but just as Matisse can convey the 'essence of cat' by a single outline of a cat whose detail we then fill in for ourselves, so Britten will express 'gull', 'wind', 'wave', 'bells', 'children', or 'storm-birds' with a clarity which enables us to point at a precise moment and say 'There!'. Where Debussy often seems intent on disguising sound by infinitely subtle blending, Britten is determined to expose it. His treatment of the individual instruments is often inventive and ingenious in the extreme, but he prefers to bring out their essential qualities rather than to distort or conceal. For example, in the rippling arpeggio already mentioned it is perfectly possible for even a mildly discerning ear to identify the three component sounds – clarinet, harp and viola; even the addition of a soft roll on a suspended cymbal does not blur the clarity of the colours.

A typically ingenious touch occurs during the 'wave' theme on the brass. The bass moves from A down a fifth to the low D. At the moment of change Britten merges a timpani roll into a roll on the bass drum. Now low D on timpani is a less than satisfactory note as the drumhead needs to be rather slack; on the other hand the bass drum, while theoretically without pitch, has the chameleon-like ability to adapt itself to its surroundings. Put it in the company of bassoons, contra-bassoon, tuba, cellos and double basses all playing a D and it will deceive the listener into believing that it is playing a D as well. The effect is not entirely illusory since the drumhead is bound to vibrate in sympathy with sound-waves being generated around it, just as the undamped strings of a piano will respond to even non-musical sounds such as the tap of a pencil on the frame.

The tripartite sequence which I have expressed as Gull—Wind—Wave is repeated in a slightly extended form before Britten, for the first time, begins to mingle them. The violins and flutes return repeatedly to E while brief snatches of the 'wind' arpeggio begin to pile up. The orchestral mixture is as before, except that isolated strokes on the cymbal suggest the splash of water. Suddenly there is a more substantial crescendo with a whirring trill on the two oboes that suggests a violent flapping of wings. The 'bird' soars up to the highest peak of its flight and then swoops down again in circling phrases. As before it is now an unsupported unison but, in a style that is characteristic of early Britten, the formation of the melody is so designed that it suggests clearly defined, if unrelated, harmonies. Thus F major glides into D major which in turn passes through B major and A flat major, the A flat then being changed enharmonically to G sharp so as to lead conveniently to the A major 'wave' that soon reappears in the brass. A brief exchange between the 'gull' motif and the 'wind' leads to a ten-bar extension of the brass theme; this time it is allowed to build into a considerable climax conveying not so much the menace as the majesty of the sea. Greater richness is given to the sound by a more purposeful use of the lower strings. A single mighty stroke on the tam-tam (gong) adds its awe-inspiring effect before the brass chords die away to nothingness. Again the violins and flutes return to that hovering E, again the breeze rustles across the marsh. The whole Interlude has been assembled from three constituents each of which has preserved an absolute integrity. The violins and flutes are concerned throughout with only the one thematic idea and its extensions; the violas, clarinets and harps have only one figuration throughout; the brass may have the widest dynamic range but in essence their texture retains the same density. In comparison to this Debussy's scoring is kaleidoscopic, a constantly shifting pattern of irresolute sounds.

2 Sunday Morning

The proper name for the flared opening at the end of a French horn (into which the player inserts his right hand) is the 'bell'. Indeed there are occasions when, for an especially resonant effect, the horns will be instructed to play with 'bells in the air'. Whether Britten thought of this possible play on words when he decided to use horns so strikingly to represent the clangour of church bells I do not know, But I well remember the delight this typically ingenious example of his scoring caused at the first performance of the opera. Rather than using actual bells, as Puccini does so romantically in *Tosca*, Britten decided to portray the clash of overtones that is inseparable from any peal. Since he clearly visualizes only a small parish church we should not be surprised that the bell tower appears to have only four bells, three main ones to ring out the summons to the Sunday morning service and a lesser one for the final reminder calculated to hurry on the laggards.

Each bell is represented by a pair of horns punching out two notes a third apart. The moment the chord has been played it is instantly suppressed, the intention being to simulate the harsh clang as the clapper strikes the bell and then the resonant hum that follows.

The impression of D major with a sharpened fourth (G sharp) is designed to suggest the slightly out-of-tune nature of church bells, the upper partials being invariably so rich that they make their presence more forcibly felt than is the case with many instruments.

Once he has set this pattern swinging on its way (which it continues to do with something of the relentless persistence of a real chime of bells), Britten introduces a contrasting ostinato in the woodwind, bright in colour and sharply defined. Flute, oboes and clarinet are in unison, their tone given a keener edge by the shriller voices of the piccolo and E flat clarinet. One may interpret this as children playing in the churchyard or, more simply, as a symbol of the clear sunny day with a brisk wind still coming in from the sea after the storm has blown itself out. (In the opera the sequence of the Interludes is different, the 'Storm' coming second, and 'Moonlight' last.) Again the scoring is notable for precision, economy and consistency. For some sixteen bars the woodwind pattern continues with only slight variations until it is broken up by a sustained trill that disappears in a flurrying scale.

At once the pattern re-forms, this time in the first violins. In support the second violins and violas, pizzicato, divide the pattern between them asymmetrically; not only does this make the parts more interesting to play but it also creates subtle variations of tone colour. While the horns persist with their tolling bells, the wind (still in unison) set up patterns that are similar to but placed in conflict with those in the strings. At times these conflicts create quite sharp dissonances, making it reasonable to assume that Britten may indeed have had the image of children playing tag in mind, especially as the passage ends with a slithering chromatic descent such as might accompany the children as an irate Rector shoos them away.

Suddenly the mood is changed. Violas and cellos together embark on a long sustained melody that anticipates Ellen Orford's opening aria in the ensuing scene:

> Glitter of waves and glitter of sunlight
> Bid us rejoice and lift our hearts on high
> Man alone has a soul to save,
> And goes to church to worship on a Sunday.

(Copyright: Boosey and Hawkes. Text by Montagu Slater.)

The words give us a considerable clue to the content of the music, the solemn melodic line deliberately being shaped like a hymn, the occasional flickering figures on flute and piccolo suggesting the 'glitter' of sunshine reflected off the surface of the water. As in the first Interlude we now find a substantial section of music built up from three clearly defined and quite separate ingredients, the central melody, dark in timbre at first but later lifted into the violins, the woodwind 'glitter', initially a solo flute but in due course reinforced by the addition of clarinets and then oboes, and, least prominent, a bass which is barely sketched in with bassoon, double basses and harp providing occasional notes, seldom more than two at a time. No attempt is made to blend these components; they simply co-exist.

A series of trills on the full strings leads to a central climax. The 'bell' motif is now more robustly scored with trombones and tuba taking the first and third bell-chime, while all four horns take the second. The brittle woodwind phrase that served as an original counterpoint to the bells is now given to strident trumpets, whose four-note pattern the strings duplicate at twice the speed. As for the wind, as one man they articulate a fidgety rhythm composed of varying numbers of repeated notes, from as few as two to as many as twelve. Although Britten is here using nearly his entire orchestra (only bassoons, harp, double-basses and percussion are silent) the formula is simplicity itself, an irregular rhythm in the woodwind, block harmonies slowly rotating between trombones and horns, and a clipped and angular phrase in the trumpets whose initial shape is reiterated at double speed in the strings. It is almost machine-like in its precision, a somewhat simplified version of the mosaic technique often employed by Stravinsky in *The Rite of Spring* – simplified because the components are fewer in number.

Three mighty clangs on bell, gong and harp lead to the dissolution of these patterns and they dissolve in a confusion of trills and scales. (Notice the characteristically brilliant use of a D trumpet to add a brassy glitter to a swift scale in the violins.) Gradually the clamour subsides. O' ce again the theme of Ellen Orford's aria emerges, now on violins at the actual pitch at which she will in due course sing it. The accompaniment is marginally less sketchy than before, the 'glitter' in the flute and piccolo being every bit as dazzling. Britten's dynamics are very positive here, *pp ma espressivo* in the violins, *ff* in the flute, *mf cresc.* and then *f cresc.* in the shriller piccolo.

As the violins come to the end of their 'verse' of Ellen's song (see p. 147 '. . . on a Sunday') a new section begins, marked by the persistent tolling of an actual bell on an E flat. Muted horns softly sustain the same note, confirming that their impersonation of bells was intended. The strings bravely continue the brisk ostinato which accompanied the first bell-chime, but it soon disintegrates and dies away to nothing. Meanwhile Britten sets out to convey the indeterminate pitch of bells in several ways. Bell-tone tends to vibrate with what tuners would call a slow 'beat'; to capture this effect Britten sets up a conflict between several adjacent semitones.

The components of this intriguing mixture can be seen as a single chord:

The B flat at the bottom of the harp chord will soon disappear; its prime purpose is to set up a resonance which the double basses then prolong, complete with F natural. This, coupled with the low D on the contra-bassoon, creates a chord of D *minor*. But if we couple that same low D to the notes given to the bassoons and oboes, we find a chord of D *major*. Against this unresolved mixture of D tonalities the E flat on bell and stopped horns sets up a real conflict. A study of the dynamics helps us to get the sound into a proper focus. The bell is *ff* and therefore truly in the foreground. (It is, one might say, Reality breaking into the Abstract.) The horns supporting it (*pp*) are little more than a stabilizer to counteract the disruptive effect of the individual strokes of the bell. The oboes and bassoons, the D major element, are marked *mf* and will sound quite positive, whereas the low F natural on double basses is *pp* and will only be felt as a vague disturbance of the harmonic equilibrium. The most subtle touch has still to be identified. It is a clarinet part which for twenty-seven bars gently oscillates between D sharp and E natural. Relate this oscillation to the reiterated E flats on the bell and you can judge the way in which it slightly blurs the sound, emphasizing the 'beat' effect.

(The clarinet part is divided between two players, one on the A clarinet, the other on the E flat.)

Meanwhile the oboes and muted trumpets, a surprisingly well-matched combination often used, continue the Ding-Dong-Dang-Dong so boldly initiated by the horns at the start of the Interlude. (See p. 145.) Now it seems faint and distant, the 'real' bell of E flat almost obliterating the synthetic chime.

Although in fact we never see the church interior in the opera, even though we hear the service in progress, the purpose of this Interlude is at least to bring us to the church-door. The strings give us a last reminder of Ellen's 'hymn' towards the end of the piece, the playful flute figure again picking up the implied reference to the glittering waters. A last insistent clanging of the bell hurries on the late-comers until, the congregation safely

149

gathered in, its noisy summons dies away, the notes separated out as the bell swings free.

Longer and more developed than the first Interlude though this may be, it still shows the same determination to limit the material to a handful of ideas, each serving an invariable purpose. If one questions this, perhaps feeling it to show a lack of fertility, it is worth considering the music within the context of a major opera. Of all musical forms, opera is the one most likely to become diffuse. The need to follow a story-line, not to mention the requirements of the text, place the composer in perpetual danger of losing control of the musical material. It was less of a problem in the days when opera was divided into neat packets of recitative, aria or ensemble. Once it became symphonic in scale, the problem of form became the bane of the operatic composer's life; even as radical an opera as Berg's *Wozzeck* is constructed to severely classical specifications, incorporating sonata form, variations, marches, dance forms and the like. In these Interludes, Britten seizes the opportunity to impose quite a severe discipline on the musical structure, allowing the sounds to be truly descriptive in themselves, but never permitting that descriptive quality to lead him astray into pictorial fantasy. If I may use an analogy which may seem a trifle crude and unromantic but which is surely apposite to the opera, the function of the Interludes is akin to those groynes which, though they may divide one section of the beach from another, prevent the erosion which would otherwise cause it to disintegrate.

3 Moonlight

The title 'Moonlight' may properly be translated as 'Clair de lune'. Nothing could better illustrate the fundamental differences between Britten and Debussy than a comparison between their two similarly named but so dissimilar compositions. Debussy sees the moon floating clear in a summer sky and improvises a miniature rhapsody that is almost indecently sensuous; Britten sees the moon reflected fitfully in the cold and steely waters of the North Sea. The music is sombre and austere, a nocturne fitted for a night in which a man will be hounded to madness and death.

The scoring at the start is consistently dark, the violins remaining silent for nearly fifty bars. A blend of bassoons, horns and the lower strings produces a sound that is intended to have something of the Stygian blackness of the sea at night if one tries to gaze down into its depths. Britten adds a footnote to the score asking that wherever the prevailing syncopated crotchet figure appears there should be a gentle swell to every beat except where he indicates otherwise. Even the words 'gentle swell' are a manifest clue as to the image he had in mind, but the movement of the water is sluggish as it is likely to be in an area where innumerable indentations finger their way into the surrounding marshland.

To start with, the music is unashamedly in E flat major, the home note of E flat being used as a sort of harmonic anchor around which the moving parts drift and eddy. The ear is at first deceived into imagining that the movement between cellos and basses (or bassoons and contra-bassoon) is going to be in parallel lines, but Britten avoids anything quite so obvious.

Horns and violas hold the 'anchor' note, bassoons and cellos provide the shifting centre part while double basses and contra-bassoon are given the somewhat more expansive bottom line. Although the opening chord is undeniably E flat major, the decision to make the fifth of the scale (B flat) the bass gives a curiously non-committal flavour to the chord and it is no surprise to find subsequent phrases drifting away into new keys. These wanderings sometimes end with a harmony calculated to give a momentary feeling of warmth as though for an instant the moon shines more brightly.

As a contrast to these tenebrous phrases Britten introduces a curiously disjointed melody scored for flutes and harp. The second flute is used as a sort of sustaining pedal, playing a consistent *pp* and marked with the single forbidding word 'cold'. (Imagine that in Debussy's *Clair de Lune*!) The scoring shows a punctilious attention to detail; the first flute part is given broken octaves, the second note being accented.

The lower note of the two is picked up and sustained by the second flute whose accentuation needs to be observed with extreme care.

Notice that the second note played here supplies the 'missing' triplet that should theoretically fill the space after the two B flats in the first flute part. The implied triplet rhythm is outlined by the harp, adding a slight glitter to the flute tone.

The third note, being a harmonic, sounds an octave higher than it is written. The combined sound is bright and clear with an unusual ricochet effect as though the sound bounces off a reflecting surface. Romantic souls may choose to interpret this as starlight, which is indeed cold, and whose twinkling light Britten may indeed have been symbolizing in this way. Subsequent events, in which this pattern rises and falls, or at times sways to and fro, lead me to suggest another image, that of the mast-tips of moored fishing-boats, picked out by the moonlight as they bob and dip at anchor.

As we have already discovered, the specific interpretation of musical images should not lead us to suppose that thereafter they will continue to behave according to material laws. Whether Britten intends this pattern to signify starlight, the tips of mastheads or even the cry of a nocturnal bird becomes irrelevant once he begins to develop it according to musical precepts. Gradually it assumes a greater importance, reducing the strings and lower wind to a static role in which they intermittently sustain a dissonant chord with strong implications of a dominant seventh in B flat. However, the flute and harp's obsessional reiteration of A natural and B natural has its effect and the strings duly yield, resuming in C major.

And now for the first time other instruments begin to insinuate themselves into the texture. A solo trombone softly proclaims a C major arpeggio which is gently contradicted by a B minor arpeggio from a solo trumpet. The rising figure is taken up by a number of instruments in turn, flute and violins (F sharp minor), tuba and double basses (A flat major), second trombone, tuba and cellos (also A flat major) and lastly trumpets in augmentation (minims instead of crotchets). By Fig. 3, approximately sixty bars into the Interlude, almost the whole orchestra has become involved. Persistent G flats coupled with the A flat arpeggios already described suggest an inevitable arrival at D flat major, but at the very moment when the resolution seems imminent the music, encouraged by a roll on the timpani, breaks through to the initial key of E flat, a climax which vividly suggests a bright moon suddenly emerging from behind a bank of clouds.

The broken octave figure shown on p. 151 reappears in harsher tones, reinforced by the brittle sound of a xylophone and with a piccolo duplicating the flute part with its characteristic shrillness. The opening music is now taken up by the the full string section divided into eleven parts, extensively doubled in wind and brass. The texture is extraordinarily opaque apart from the sharp-edged interpolations from flute, piccolo, xylophone and harp. While one is perhaps made aware of the immensity of sea and sky, one also gains the impression that the elements are impersonal and unforgiving. Although for the most part the dynamic in strings, wind and brass is *p*, the sheer weight of sound is crushing, its sombre quality enhanced by surging rumbles from the timpani. At last a climax is reached (Fig. 4) in which strings and wind freeze on a long-held dissonance against which the flute-piccolo-harp-xylophone combination, now reinforced with the small D trumpet, begins a long and tortuous descent. Little by little the sound diminishes until only the five instruments specified above are left. For a few bars they oscillate gently on two adjacent notes; indeed, we think that the piece may well finish at this point. Instead, Britten re-introduces a quiet recollection of the opening phrase, scored as before, but now seeming gentler by contrast with the preceding climax. A final confirmation of E flat major from the lower strings (still with the collaboration of bassoon, two horns and contrabassoon) dies away. Now nothing is left but three last flickers of light from flute, harp and piccolo, each marked with a cautionary *ppp*.

As in the previous Interludes, the music is notable for its economy and consistency; here there are only two musical elements to take into consideration and yet when we come to the end we feel that we have experienced a substantial movement conceived on a genuinely symphonic scale. It is the very tenacity with which Britten adheres to only two basic patterns that gives the music its span. It moves with grave inevitability towards one considerable central climax and then recedes. The structure could scarcely be more simple; we shall find a rather more complex scheme in the final Interlude.

4 Storm

Confronted with the task of writing storm music, any composer is forced to accept that certain orchestral clichés are almost unavoidable. There is no better way of imitating thunder than to use drums; a howling wind does make a chromatic wail; torrential rain does not fall in slow motion. The avoidance of such clichés, however desirable, may come to seem merely perverse; their inclusion lays the writer open to the accusation of plagiarism. It is not hard to write music that is full of sound and fury; the problem is to make is signify something.

To drag Britten's storm out of the context of the opera is not wholly fair since the first mutterings from which it is destined to grow are laid well in advance. Many pages before the storm bursts into its full fury certain crucial motives appear. The relevance of one is immediately established by the words 'Look, the storm cone!', sung by the retired sea-captain Balstrode.

A mere eleven bars later a modified version of this fragment becomes the subject of an immensely dramatic choral fugue whose exposition is ingeniously worked out on solo voices while the chorus provides excitable counterpoint virtually in speech rhythm.

Balstrode's theme, as shown above, is duly taken up by the chorus, men and women in turn, while the soloists now provide a babble of excitement. The whole ensemble is worked out with complete mastery. Periodically the orchestra hammers out a syncopated rhythm with a sharp dissonance at its centre:

The clash E flat—C sharp is created by a shift in contrary motion from the unison D. A fervent cry goes up from everyone on stage exploiting and extending the same pattern.

By combining this type of harmonic clash with the 'shape' of the fugue subject, Britten produces the basic material of his orchestral storm.

The Interlude may therefore be regarded as an orchestral fantasy based on a choral theme. Much use is made of the clash of a tone created by a contrary motion divergence from a single central note; it is a pattern from which Britten is easily able to derive the chromatic 'wailing' of the wind, though it says much for his strength of mind that not once in the entire Interlude does he employ the tremolando bowing that string players expect as a matter of course in all such pieces.

154

The scoring in the first few bars is mostly for the lower strings supported by clarinets and bassoons. The outer notes of the pattern are heavily underlined by the horns, while even the timpani player has some support from isolated bass notes on the harp; they may not be all that audible amongst the general hubbub, but they do help to focus the pitch of the kettledrums more accurately.

In the sixth bar we find a new figure developing whose upward thrust suggests the build-up of huge waves. While the activity may seem to be concentrated in the wind and strings, it is the horns that provide a tough central core to the harmony. Notice that Britten keeps plenty in reserve in the early stages, trumpets, trombones, percussion, flutes, oboes and first violins all being silent for the first few bars. At Fig. 1 the pitch is raised an octave with the violins beginning to exploit the rich tension of the G string, and the first sporadic blasts from the trumpet. The cumulative 'wave-building' phrase is next pitched an octave and a half higher with the trumpets adding their considerable weight and brilliance to the horns. By the time he reaches Fig. 2, some nineteen bars from the beginning, Britten is using virtually a full orchestra, only the trombones, tuba and (amazingly) the percussion still being left out. Although this means that eighteen instruments plus the full complement of strings are now playing, the actual musical content can be reduced to a mere four elements:

(i)

which is played by flutes, oboes and all the violins at the same pitch;

(ii)

shared by clarinets and violas;

(iii)

which is allotted to the bassoons and cellos;

(iv)

given to timpani, harp and pizzicato double basses.

The contra-bassoon and tuba reinforce the initial E flat that begins each bar, while horns and trumpets between them present a rhythmically distorted variant of (iii). I have a letter from Britten saying of the score of *Peter Grimes* that 'It's really very simple', and, looking at the components that go to make up this seemingly complex mosaic of sound one can understand what he meant. Despite the impression of near-chaotic frenzy everything is planned with absolute precision.

A downward rush in strings and wind leads to a brief re-statement of (i), but just as we think we are in for a full-scale repetition, the trombones make their long-awaited entrance. Some commentators claim that they are alluding to part of the 'Wave' theme from Interlude 1, but I prefer to see it as a distortion of the phrase with which, in the immediately preceding scene, Grimes had declared his intention to marry Ellen. There is an exciting rapid-fire duet between Grimes and Balstrode whose main thematic element is this pattern:

Three times Grimes declaims this phrase in augmentation of the words 'I'll marry Ellen!'

It isn't too far-fetched to see the trombone-phrase in the storm as a mad distortion of this:

in other words the storm rages in Grimes's mind as well as in the elements. The relationship may have emanated from the sub-conscious, but since the storm is linked directly to the previous scene, and since elsewhere in the Interlude Britten makes two extensive allusions to that scene, I am not theorizing wildly.

What is indisputable is yet more evidence of the essential clarity of the scoring. Once again he has reduced the music to two basic ideas, the tight-packed triadic harmonies in the trombones and the uneasy and disturbing bass-line forcefully played by bassoons, contra-bassoon, cellos and double basses.

Occasional rumbles from the bass drum (focussed onto a note by horns, tuba and harp) are little more than a sound effect.

After six bars, the trumpets take over the trombones' theme until a musical trial of strength between them gives the impression of a flood-tide building up until all restraining barriers are smashed. The opening idea bursts in once again, though not quite at full strength since it is given to strings only without the skirl of the woodwind to add bite. Britten is anxious not to drown (well-chosen word!) an important new element that sails arrogantly through the turbulent string passages, magnificently scored for four horns in unison at the octave. It leads us towards a change of tempo (Fig. 7) and a shrill outburst from all the upper woodwind in unison, circling and swooping in such a way that it has been suggested that it represents not the howl of the tempest but a scurrying flight of petrels or skuas skimming over the wave-crests in wild abandon. The two piccolos Britten uses at this point give the music an ear-splitting shrillness that more than compensates for the loss of the heavy brass.

Throughout the movement so far, Britten has been extraordinarily reticent in his use of percussion other than the bass drum and timpani. Here, though, we find the side-drum being used to good effect in single beats, perhaps as though a shutter had broken loose and was banging against a window-frame. Cymbals clashed for the first time help to reintroduce the initial theme, now scored for bassoons, trombones and the lower strings. It is the most violent setting of all, with several new rhythmic complexities and the baying of the trombones adding an even greater ferocity. Such a climax too long extended could become self-defeating; within a matter of eight bars Britten begins a prolonged descent, sustained chords in the wind, repeated quavers in the strings, over a long-held low F from timpani, cellos and basses. Even the tempo gradually slackens in pace.

The low F slides down a semitone to an E natural (double basses, contra-bassoon and bass-drum) whereupon there is a breathtaking change of mood. Ushered in with a harp glissando and lusciously scored for unison strings over a rich brass chord, one of the most memorable and significant phrases in the whole opera makes its romantic entrance. It first appeared in the scene before the storm as Grimes gazes out towards the threatening horizon seeking some release from his troubled thoughts.

This phrase, with its yearning ninth, smooth descent and choppy aftermath, now reappears in orchestral guise, a high trill in the wind suggesting the white glare that sometimes appears in great storms as the black clouds drift apart before gathering with renewed menace. The moment of stillness does not last; it is interrupted by four bars of chattering quavers that toy with a corrupted version of A major. Again there is a moment of stillness, again the visionary phrase orchestrated as before. The chattering response dies away for a second time. Once more there is a harp glissando and we wonder if the haunting phrase is going to unwind yet again. It is not to be, for though he may pray for peace, peace will not come to Grimes. The woodwind set up a restless syncopated figure that is matched by tambourine and double basses. Centred on A, it keeps nudging the adjacent semitones B flat and G sharp. Meanwhile the strings tenderly unfold layer by layer another phrase whose significance is clarified by referring to the previous scene. Grimes, realizing that Ellen alone can bring some solace to his twisted mind, dreams of sharing his life with her.

It is this phrase that the strings tenderly recall while the woodwind's fidgety and dissonant syncopations tell us that Grimes will never know the solace he yearns for.

For the fourth and last time the harp glissando leads the strings into their arc of melody, for the fourth time it is cut off by the busy patter of quavers, this time gradually descending through a corrupted version of A major. The music dies to a true *pp*. Suddenly, as the storm music resumes, we realize that the dancing quavers are spattering raindrops. Urgent but suppressed figuration in the strings tells us that the rain is falling in earnest now. (Fig. 12) The storm motif appears in augmentation in the woodwind:

Low trombones grumble threateningly as the music gathers impetus. We have been in the eye of the storm and soon it will swirl around us once again. A sudden crescendo gusts; an extraordinarily shrill figure for virtually full orchestra suggests the howling gale sweeping all before it. A skidding chromatic descent through two octaves is possibly explained by a line in the ensuing scene when a fisherman reports that 'there's been a landslide up the coast'. With three massive abrupt chords Britten slams the music to a stop. Even to the end the texture has remained stark. The interested listener should try the experiment of listening first to Debussy's 'Dialogue du vent et de la mer' from his orchestral suite *La Mer* and then to Britten's 'Storm'. Only then will he appreciate the full extent of the revolutionary change that had taken place in attitudes to the orchestra. Debussy's score will certainly seem the more attractive, the more varied in colour. It was precisely because Debussy (and some of his contemporaries) had made orchestral sound so seductive that Britten had, as it were, to cleanse the palate. It would be absurd to suggest that Britten was in any way incompetent as an orchestrator. As a boy of fourteen he had written some French songs with orchestral accompaniment that are as ravishingly beautiful in sonority as Debussy or Ravel at their best. However, someone of his originality would not be content merely to reproduce textures already fully explored. He had to find his own way; in doing so he decided to strip off what might be termed the cosmetics of scoring and reveal the unadorned truth about sound. In some of the later chamber operas his ingenuity in scoring for a small orchestra can seldom have been surpassed. Financial reasons apart, he must by nature have welcomed the challenge of writing for a group too small in numbers to allow any 'padding'. 'Clarity is paramount' might have served him as a motto; if a thing can't be heard it's not worth writing down. It is a precept that is admirably illustrated by the *Sea Interludes*.

Coda

Although the language of music has undergone many radical changes in the course of history, none has been so fundamental as the one experienced during the last three decades. The introduction of electronic sound, at first regarded as little more than a toy, has hugely enlarged the composer's resources. He is now able if he wishes to eliminate the performer entirely by producing a definitive master-tape himself. Nevertheless, audiences are not greatly satisfied by the prospect of listening to machines; the live performer still has a worth while contribution to make even if it is only to give the public something to look at. The synthesizer, like the computer, is a servant rather than a master. It can provide a wealth of new sounds as well as distorting the tones of familiar instruments in such a way as to change their character entirely. To disregard so versatile and novel a tool would be folly, but since it lacks both mind and soul it is incapable of true invention. The man who uses it needs to be a new type of musician, one who is at home in a world where science, mathematics and electronic engineering are as much a part of his training as counterpoint, harmony and form were to earlier generations. It is hardly surprising that since the sounds themselves are largely unfamiliar, they are best suited to express the paranormal. Once we have actually seen man walk upon the moon, the 'Moonlight' music of Debussy or Britten will no longer be adequate to express our reaction; we *need* music that will literally sound unearthly.

If synthesizers were at some future date to become our sole source of music, I would view the prospect with despair. Fortunately there is little sign of them totally displacing the orchestra, although there are composers who vow that the symphony orchestra of today is an anachronism that belongs in a cultural museum. To counter this accusation (which partly reflects the political beliefs of the anti-bourgeoisie), composers have experimented with the idea of dismantling it and re-arranging its components. For example in his *Concerto for orchestra* Michael Tippett divides his resources into three groups. The first, whose function is to provide music of 'line and flow', consists of flute, harp, tuba, piano and three horns; the second, for 'rhythm and dynamic punch' (Tippett's own phrases), mixes timpani and piano, oboe, cor anglais, bassoon, contra-bassoon, two trombones and percussion;

160

the third group, chosen for 'virtuosity and speed', matches piano and xylophone, clarinet and bass clarinet, two trumpets and side-drum. It will be observed that only the piano participates in all three groups. Where then are the strings, the traditional backbone of the orchestra? The answer is 'Nowhere', at least in the first movement. Their recompense for this slight, such as it is, comes in the second movement, which is scored for strings, piano and harp; this time it is the woodwind and brass who are put into Coventry, forced for once to sit back and listen to their colleagues. (Orchestral players are notorious for welcoming any excuse to leave the platform, but in this case they can scarcely make a mass exodus only to return later to play the finale.) The combination of what is in effect three chamber orchestras of a curiously mixed kind presents both listeners and performers with a new challenge.

In Thea Musgrave's clarinet concerto the orchestra is similarly divided into a number of groups to whom the soloist pays periodic 'visits', literally walking from point to point on the stage so as to identify with each sound-complex in turn. Such experiments are not only perfectly legitimate but may be regarded as historically inevitable.

Certainly there came a time in this century when the orchestra showed signs of becoming grotesquely over-inflated. Schoenberg's early and hyper-Romantic work, the *Gurrelieder*, requires an orchestra of such immensity that few platforms could accommodate it. In addition to 5 solo singers and a narrator, he called for 3 four-part male voice choirs, an eight-part mixed choir, 4 piccolos, 4 flutes, 3 oboes, 2 cor anglais (also doubling on oboe), 7 clarinets including the small E flat clarinet and the large bass clarinet, 3 bassoons, 2 contra-bassoons, 10 horns, 6 trumpets, 1 bass trumpet, 1 alto trombone, 4 tenor trombones, 2 bass trombones, 1 tuba, a vast percussion section including 6 timpani, 4 harps, celesta and not less than 85 strings. Such works, apart from exhibiting a sort of musical elephantiasis, have virtually priced themselves out of the market. Naturally enough the sound is magnificent – one could hardly fail with such resources at one's disposal.

Curiously enough Webern, a self-denying composer if ever there was one, employed nearly as vast an orchestra in his early compositions before turning his back on such extravagant displays in favour of an etiolated austerity that was to fascinate a whole new generation of composers. It has been said of Webern that he discovered the expressive power of the single note. A pianist can only create an expressive sound at the moment of impact of hammer on string; after that he is powerless to modify the sound in any way except by adding further notes. His ability to play expressively depends on a fine judgement of the tonal balance between consecutive notes – in a phrase, on 'tone gradation'. None of the instruments in the orchestra except the harp and a few members of the percussion family suffers from this handicap. Any wind, string or brass instrument can make a single note express a wide emotional range from aggression to extreme tenderness. Webern became fascinated by this ability, even going to far as to orchestrate the six-part Ricercare from Bach's *Musical Offering* in such a way that each note of the fugue-subject was allocated to a different instrument. It was an experiment designed to force the listener to change his listening habits, experiencing each note as an 'event' in its own right rather than as one link in a chain.

Now it is undeniable that a great deal of contempory music presents problems to the listener. Traditional harmonic procedures are anathema to the composer; new forms have been devised, often drawn from the extra-musical worlds of geometry, architecture or mathematics. To many people this seems retrogressive, the irony being that music of the greatest sophis-tication is regarded as barbarous. If it is true that melody in the conventional sense, that is to say 'singable' melody, has lost its appeal for the serious composer, and if it is true that harmony (in the traditional sense of con-sonance) has also been banished, what is left? Rhythm and Texture. Rhythm has been enormously developed in our century as the multiple time-signatures in scores by Stravinsky or Bartók clearly show. As for Texture, by which I mean the combination of sounds of a different colour, it is an area that has been much cultivated. Sonority, tone-colour, call it what you will, has become an obsession with the contempory composer. He is fascinated by sound as an abstract entity. Orchestration today is not a matter of trans-cribing for orchestra something originally conceived at the keyboard. We have learned that sound can be compelling on its own. (As corroboration of that statement I would cite the huge expansion of interest in percussion, the area of the orchestra least exploited by our nineteenth-century forefathers.)

If we are baffled by modern music it is often because we are listening to it in the wrong way, searching for recognizable themes that ought duly to reappear in new guises. Trained to expect a sequence of related events we lose our bearings in the absence of structural landmarks. I can think of no more helpful advice than to urge the listener to concentrate on the orchestra-tion, to savour the relative values of different sounds. To give a very simple example, not even drawn from the orchestral repertoire, Shostakovich begins his piano trio with quite a lengthy phrase for solo cello. The notes specified are all harmonics which not only makes the cellist seem to be trespassing on the violinist's preserves but which also have a strangely ethereal quality quite unlike what one is expecting from a cello. The identi-cal notes played comfortably on a violin would not have the same effect. It is not the theme that catches our attention so much as the *sound* of the theme. This is no modern phenomenon; think of the opening notes of Weber's *Oberon* overture – three consecutive notes of the scale but totally magical as *sound* because of the choice of instrument; not a cello, not a clarinet, not the first violins nor the violas, but a single horn, hand-stopped to make it seem incredibly distant. Turn for comparison to the opening theme of Schubert's

'Great' C major symphony. That too begins with three rising notes of a scale, but how different the sound is. The horn is no longer mysterious and magical, but noble and commanding. Here we do listen to the theme rather than to the sound it makes, and when it is transferred to other instruments we don't bewail the loss of the horn. Far from it; we welcome the chance of hearing the tune again and revel in the harmonies that Schubert now offers in support. The two works, even though roughly contemporary with each other, make different demands upon the listener, demands which are clarified by the orchestration.

Sound is almost impossible to describe; try to explain verbally the difference between a cello and a violin playing the same note and one is at a loss for words; even to differentiate between a flute and a violin would be difficult. In this respect any book about the 'sounds of music' is bound to be a failure unless author and reader are sharing a common memory. We learn how to tell a flute from a violin by remembering their respective sounds. It is for this reason that I have chosen to write about works that are widely known, hoping to kindle a response through shared experience. As I have said before, this is not a textbook on How to Orchestrate; its sole purpose is to encourage more perceptive listening, for that is the road to a keener enjoyment of music's delights. If at times the process has seemed a trifle laboured, I would remind you of the immense labour involved in actually writing out an orchestral score. That labour was not only physical, even cripplingly so in some cases; it was also mental, involving the uncanny ability to imagine sound in depth. Surely it is only fair that we should learn to work a little harder at our listening when composers of extraordinary genius have laboured so hard on our behalf?

Some Suggestions for Further Listening

Mozart	Serenade in C minor for 13 wind instruments.
Mendelssohn	Scherzo from the Octet for strings. Compare with his own orchestral version in the First Symphony.
Mendelssohn	Scherzo from *A Midsummer Night's Dream*. Compare with the brilliant piano transcription made by Rakhmaninov.
Tchaikovsky	Serenade in C for strings. Masterly use of string orchestra, to be compared with Mozart above.
Tchaikovsky	Symphony No. 4, Scherzo. Neatly divides into pizzicato strings, woodwind and then brass in sequence.
Rimsky-Korsakoff	*Capriccio Espagnole*. Plenty of clearly defined solos for the players in a virtuoso score.
Wagner	*The Mastersingers* Overture, to be compared with
Wagner	*Siegfried Idyll*. Delicacy as opposed to fullness of sound.
Brahms	*Variations on the St.Antoni Chorale*. Compare the version for two pianos with the orchestral version.
Richard Strauss	*'Don Juan'*. An extravagant score that demands the utmost from the players. A complex ear-test.
Delius	*Brigg Fair*. A hauntingly beautiful set of variations on a Lincolnshire folk-song.
Kodály	*Dances of Galanta*. An important part for a solo clarinet plus some wonderful gipsy-style fiddling.
Ravel-Mussorgsky	*Pictures from an Exhibition*, to be compared with Mussorgsky's original version for piano solo.
Ravel	*Valses Nobles et Sentimentales*. Originally for piano; orchestrated by the composer. Compare the two versions.

Ravel *Le Tombeau de Couperin*. Another Ravel work that exists in two authentic versions, one for piano, one for orchestra.

Stravinsky *Firebird* ⎫

Stravinsky *Petrushka* ⎬ Taken in this order one can see the composer's individuality growing.

Stravinsky *The Rite of Spring* ⎭

Prokofiev *Classical Symphony*. Scored for an eighteenth-century-size orchestra, it is notable for extraordinary clarity. To be compared with

Stravinsky *Pulcinella*. Another work using a small orchestra to brilliant effect.

Respighi *The Birds*. Charming transcriptions of tunes from earlier centuries; deft use of a small orchestra.

Bartók Concerto for Orchestra ⎫ Two examples of

Lutosławski Concerto for Orchestra ⎬ twentieth-century virtuosity in orchestral writing.

Panufnik *Nocturne for orchestra*. One of the most beautiful of all modern works in its use of pure sound.

Index

169

Index